LOW OXALATE COOKBOOK

3 Manuscripts in 1 – 120+ Low oxalate - friendly recipes including Pizza, Salad, and Casseroles for a delicious and tasty diet

TABLE OF CONTENTS

Introduction

Low Oxalate recipes for personal enjoyment but also for family enjoyment. You will love them for sure for how easy it is to prepare them.

BOOK 1

40+Stew, Roast and Casserole recipes for a healthy and balanced Low oxalate diet

ROAST RECIPES:

LOW-OXALATE HERB-ROASTED CHICKEN

Serves: 4
Prep time: 10 Minutes
Total time: 1 hour 30 Minutes

INGREDIENTS

- 1 whole low-oxalate chicken (about 3-4 pounds)
- 2 tablespoons low-oxalate olive oil
- 2 teaspoons low-oxalate dried herbs (e.g., thyme, rosemary, oregano)
- 1 teaspoon low-oxalate garlic powder
- Salt and pepper, to taste

DIRECTIONS

1. Preheat the oven to 375°F (190°C) and coat a roasting pan with cooking spray.
2. Clean and pat dry the chicken with paper towels.
3. Spread the olive oil all over the chicken to coat it evenly.
4. In a small mixing bowl, combine the dry herbs, garlic powder, salt, and pepper.
5. Spread the herb mixture all over the chicken, massaging it in.
6. Put the bird in a roasting pan that has been oiled.
7. Cook for about 1 hour and 30 Minutes, or until the internal temperature reaches 165°F (74°C) and the skin is golden brown and crispy.

8. Take the chicken from the oven and set it aside for 10 Minutes to rest before carving.
9. With your choice of side dishes, serve the low-oxalate herb-roasted chicken.

NUTRITIONAL FACTS (PER SERVING)

Calories: 320
Protein: 27g
Carbohydrates: 0g
Fat: 22g

LOW-OXALATE BALSAMIC ROASTED VEGETABLES

Serves: 4
Prep time: 15 Minutes
Total time: 45 Minutes

INGREDIENTS

- 2 cups low-oxalate mixed vegetables (e.g., carrots, bell peppers, zucchini, eggplant), cut into bite-sized pieces
- 2 tablespoons low-oxalate balsamic vinegar
- 2 tablespoons low-oxalate olive oil
- 2 cloves low-oxalate garlic, minced
- 1 teaspoon low-oxalate dried herbs (e.g., thyme, rosemary)
- Salt and pepper, to taste

DIRECTIONS

1. Preheat the oven to 400 degrees Fahrenheit (200 degrees Celsius) and line a baking sheet with parchment paper.
2. Whisk together the balsamic vinegar, olive oil, minced garlic, dried herbs, salt, and pepper in a mixing bowl.
3. Toss the mixed veggies in the bowl with the balsamic mixture to coat.
4. Distribute the vegetables evenly on the baking sheet.
5. Roast the vegetables in a warm oven for 30-35 Minutes, or until soft and slightly caramelised, stirring halfway through.
6. Remove from the oven and set aside to cool slightly before serving.
7. Serve the low-oxalate balsamic roasted vegetables with your favourite protein as a side dish.

NUTRITIONAL FACTS (PER SERVING)

Calories: 120
Protein: 2g
Carbohydrates: 10g
Fat: 9g

LOW-OXALATE ROAST BEEF WITH GRAVY

Serves: 6
Prep time: 15 Minutes
Total time: 2 hours

INGREDIENTS

- 2 pounds low-oxalate beef roast (e.g., sirloin, tenderloin)
- 2 tablespoons low-oxalate olive oil
- 2 teaspoons low-oxalate garlic powder
- 2 teaspoons low-oxalate dried herbs (e.g., thyme, rosemary)
- Salt and pepper, to taste
- 2 cups low-oxalate beef broth
- 2 tablespoons low-oxalate cornstarch (optional, for thickening)

DIRECTIONS

1. Preheat the oven to 325°F (160°C) and coat a roasting pan with cooking spray.
2. Coat the beef roast in olive oil, garlic powder, dried herbs, salt, and pepper to cover evenly.
3. Put the beef roast in a roasting pan that has been oiled.
4. Roast for 1 hour and 30 Minutes, or until the internal temperature achieves your preferred level of doneness (e.g., 135°F (57°C) for medium-rare, 145°F (63°C) for medium).
5. Take the beef roast from the oven and set aside for 15 Minutes to rest before slicing.
6. Prepare the gravy while the beef is resting. Warm the beef broth in a saucepan over medium heat.
7. If preferred, make a slurry of the cornflour and a tiny quantity of water, then whisk it into the simmering soup to

thicken the gravy. Simmer for a few Minutes, or until the sauce has thickened.

8. Serve the beef roast sliced with the gravy.

NUTRITIONAL FACTS (PER SERVING)

Calories: 280
Protein: 40g
Carbohydrates: 2g
Fat: 11g

LOW-OXALATE LEMON HERB ROASTED SALMON

Serves: 4
Prep time: 10 Minutes
Total time: 25 Minutes

INGREDIENTS

- 4 low-oxalate salmon fillets (about 6 ounces each)
- 2 tablespoons low-oxalate olive oil
- Juice and zest of 1 lemon
- 2 teaspoons low-oxalate dried herbs (e.g., dill, thyme)
- Salt and pepper, to taste

DIRECTIONS

1. Preheat the oven to 425 degrees Fahrenheit (220 degrees Celsius) and line a baking sheet with parchment paper.
2. Put the salmon fillets on the baking sheet that has been prepared.
3. Whisk together the olive oil, lemon juice, lemon zest, dried herbs, salt, and pepper in a small bowl.
4. Spread the lemon herb mixture evenly over the salmon fillets.
5. Cook for 12-15 Minutes, or until the salmon is cooked to your chosen level of doneness, in a preheated oven.
6. Take the roasted salmon from the oven and set aside for a few Minutes before serving.
7. Serve the low-oxalate lemon herb grilled salmon with roasted vegetables or a salad as a side dish.

NUTRITIONAL FACTS (PER SERVING)

Calories: 350
Protein: 34g
Carbohydrates: 1g
Fat: 24g

LOW-OXALATE ROASTED TURKEY BREAST

Serves: 6
Prep time: 15 Minutes
Total time: 2 hours

INGREDIENTS

- 3 pounds low-oxalate boneless turkey breast
- 2 tablespoons low-oxalate olive oil
- 2 teaspoons low-oxalate garlic powder
- 2 teaspoons low-oxalate dried herbs (e.g., sage, thyme, rosemary)
- Salt and pepper, to taste
- 1 cup low-oxalate chicken broth

DIRECTIONS

1. Preheat the oven to 325°F (160°C) and coat a roasting pan with cooking spray.
2. Put the turkey breast in a roasting pan that has been oiled.
3. Combine the olive oil, garlic powder, dried herbs, salt, and pepper in a small bowl.
4. Make sure the turkey breast is evenly coated with the herb mixture.
5. Fill the roasting pan halfway with chicken broth.
6. Roast for about 1 hour and 30 Minutes, or until the internal temperature reaches 165°F (74°C) and the turkey is cooked through.
7. Take the turkey breast from the oven and set aside for 15 Minutes to rest before slicing.

8. With your choice of side dishes, serve the low-oxalate roasted turkey breast.

NUTRITIONAL FACTS (PER SERVING)

Calories: 250
Protein: 45g
Carbohydrates: 0g
Fat: 7g

LOW-OXALATE ROASTED PORK TENDERLOIN

Serves: 4
Prep time: 10 Minutes
Total time: 30 Minutes

INGREDIENTS

- 1 pound low-oxalate pork tenderloin
- 2 tablespoons low-oxalate olive oil
- 2 teaspoons low-oxalate garlic powder
- 2 teaspoons low-oxalate dried herbs (e.g., thyme, rosemary)
- Salt and pepper, to taste

DIRECTIONS

1. Preheat the oven to 400°F (200°C) and coat a roasting pan with cooking spray.
2. Put the pork tenderloin in a roasting pan that has been oiled.
3. Combine the olive oil, garlic powder, dried herbs, salt, and pepper in a small bowl.
4. Make sure the pork tenderloin is evenly coated with the herb mixture.
5. Cook for 20-25 Minutes in a preheated oven, or until the internal temperature reaches 145°F (63°C) and the pork is cooked through.
6. Take the pork tenderloin from the oven and set aside for 5 Minutes to rest before slicing.
7. With your choice of side dishes, serve the low-oxalate roasted pork tenderloin.

NUTRITIONAL FACTS (PER SERVING)

Calories: 200
Protein: 30g
Carbohydrates: 0g
Fat: 9g

LOW-OXALATE HERB-CRUSTED ROAST BEEF

Serves: 8
Prep time: 15 Minutes
Total time: 2 hours 30 Minutes

INGREDIENTS

- 3 pounds low-oxalate beef roast (e.g., sirloin, ribeye)
- 2 tablespoons low-oxalate Dijon mustard
- 2 tablespoons low-oxalate olive oil
- 2 teaspoons low-oxalate dried herbs (e.g., thyme, rosemary)
- 2 teaspoons low-oxalate garlic powder
- Salt and pepper, to taste

DIRECTIONS

1. Preheat the oven to 325°F (160°C) and coat a roasting pan with cooking spray.
2. Whisk together the Dijon mustard, olive oil, dried herbs, garlic powder, salt, and pepper in a small bowl.
3. Put the beef roast in a roasting pan that has been oiled.
4. Cover the top and sides of the meat roast with the herb mixture.
5. Roast for about 2 hours, or until the internal temperature reaches your preferred level of doneness (for example, 135°F (57°C) for medium-rare, 145°F (63°C) for medium).
6. Take the beef roast from the oven and set aside for 15 Minutes to rest before slicing.
7. Serve the herb-crusted roast beef with gravy and your favourite side dishes.

NUTRITIONAL FACTS (PER SERVING)

Calories: 320
Protein: 45g
Carbohydrates: 0g
Fat: 14g

SOUP RECIPES:

LOW-OXALATE VEGETABLE SOUP

Serves: 4
Prep time: 15 Minutes
Total time: 45 Minutes

INGREDIENTS

- 1 tablespoon low-oxalate olive oil
- 1 medium low-oxalate onion, diced
- 2 cloves low-oxalate garlic, minced
- 2 medium low-oxalate carrots, diced
- 2 medium low-oxalate celery stalks, diced
- 1 medium low-oxalate zucchini, diced
- 4 cups low-oxalate vegetable broth
- 1 cup low-oxalate diced tomatoes (canned or fresh)
- 1 teaspoon low-oxalate dried herbs (e.g., thyme, oregano)
- Salt and pepper, to taste

DIRECTIONS

1. Warm the olive oil in a big pot over medium heat.
2. Sauté the diced onion and minced garlic until aromatic and translucent in the pot.
3. Cook for a few Minutes, until the carrots, celery and zucchini are slightly softened, in the pot.
4. Pour in the veggie broth, diced tomatoes, and dried herbs.
5. Season to taste with salt and pepper.
6. Bring the soup to a boil, then reduce to a low heat and cook for 20-30 Minutes, or until the veggies are soft.
7. If required, adjust the seasonings.

8. Serve the low-oxalate vegetable soup hot, garnished as desired.

NUTRITIONAL FACTS (PER SERVING)

Calories: 90
Protein: 3g
Carbohydrates: 15g
Fat: 3g

LOW-OXALATE CHICKEN NOODLE SOUP

Serves: 4
Prep time: 10 Minutes
Total time: 40 Minutes

INGREDIENTS

- 1 tablespoon low-oxalate olive oil
- 1 medium low-oxalate onion, diced
- 2 cloves low-oxalate garlic, minced
- 2 medium low-oxalate carrots, sliced
- 2 medium low-oxalate celery stalks, sliced
- 4 cups low-oxalate chicken broth
- 2 cups low-oxalate cooked chicken breast, shredded
- 1 cup low-oxalate egg noodles (or low-oxalate alternative)
- 1 teaspoon low-oxalate dried thyme
- Salt and pepper, to taste

DIRECTIONS

1. Warm the olive oil in a big pot over medium heat.
2. Sauté the diced onion and minced garlic until aromatic and translucent in the pot.
3. Cook for a few Minutes, until the carrots and celery are slightly softened, in the pot.
4. Bring the chicken broth to a boil in a saucepan.
5. Reduce to a low heat and stir in the shredded chicken, egg noodles, dried thyme, salt, and pepper.
6. Let the soup to simmer for 15-20 Minutes, or until the noodles are al dente and the flavours have combined.
7. If required, adjust the seasonings.
8. Serve the low-oxalate chicken noodle soup hot, garnished if desired with fresh parsley.

NUTRITIONAL FACTS (PER SERVING)

Calories: 200
Protein: 20g
Carbohydrates: 15g
Fat: 6g

LOW-OXALATE BUTTERNUT SQUASH SOUP

Serves: 4
Prep time: 15 Minutes
Total time: 1 hour

INGREDIENTS

- 1 medium low-oxalate butternut squash, peeled, seeded, and cubed
- 1 medium low-oxalate onion, chopped
- 2 cloves low-oxalate garlic, minced
- 1 tablespoon low-oxalate olive oil
- 4 cups low-oxalate vegetable broth
- 1 teaspoon low-oxalate dried sage
- 1/2 teaspoon low-oxalate ground nutmeg
- Salt and pepper, to taste

DIRECTIONS

1. Preheat the oven to 400 degrees Fahrenheit (200 degrees Celsius).
2. Drizzle olive oil over the diced butternut squash on a baking sheet.
3. Season with salt and pepper to taste.
4. Roast the butternut squash for 25-30 Minutes, or until soft and slightly caramelised, in a preheated oven.
5. Warm the olive oil in a big pot over medium heat.
6. Sauté the chopped onion and minced garlic until aromatic and transparent in the pot.
7. Add the roasted butternut squash, vegetable broth, dried sage, and grated nutmeg to the pot.
8. Bring the soup to a boil, then reduce to a low heat and leave to cook for 15-20 Minutes.

9. Puree the soup with an immersion blender or in a blender until smooth.
10. If required, adjust the seasonings.
11. Serve the low-oxalate butternut squash soup warm, topped with ground nutmeg or fresh sage leaves.

NUTRITIONAL FACTS (PER SERVING)

Calories: 120
Protein: 2g
Carbohydrates: 25g
Fat: 3g

LOW-OXALATE TOMATO BASIL SOUP

Serves: 4
Prep time: 10 Minutes
Total time: 30 Minutes

INGREDIENTS

- 1 tablespoon low-oxalate olive oil
- 1 medium low-oxalate onion, diced
- 2 cloves low-oxalate garlic, minced
- 2 cups low-oxalate diced tomatoes (canned or fresh)
- 2 cups low-oxalate tomato sauce
- 2 cups low-oxalate vegetable broth
- 1/4 cup low-oxalate fresh basil leaves, chopped
- Salt and pepper, to taste

DIRECTIONS

1. Warm the olive oil in a big pot over medium heat.
2. Sauté the diced onion and minced garlic until aromatic and translucent in the pot.
3. To the pot, add the diced tomatoes, tomato sauce, and vegetable broth.
4. Bring the mixture to a boil, then reduce to a low heat and continue to cook for 15-20 Minutes.
5. Season with salt and pepper to taste after adding the basil leaves.
6. Puree the soup with an immersion blender or in a blender until smooth.
7. If required, adjust the seasonings.

8. Serve the low-oxalate tomato basil soup hot with a few fresh basil leaves on top.

NUTRITIONAL FACTS (PER SERVING)

Calories: 100
Protein: 2g
Carbohydrates: 15g
Fat: 4g

LOW-OXALATE LENTIL SOUP

Serves: 4
Prep time: 10 Minutes
Total time: 1 hour 15 Minutes

INGREDIENTS

- 1 cup low-oxalate green or brown lentils, rinsed and drained
- 1 tablespoon low-oxalate olive oil
- 1 medium low-oxalate onion, diced
- 2 cloves low-oxalate garlic, minced
- 2 medium low-oxalate carrots, diced
- 2 medium low-oxalate celery stalks, diced
- 4 cups low-oxalate vegetable broth
- 1 teaspoon low-oxalate ground cumin
- 1/2 teaspoon low-oxalate ground coriander
- 1/4 teaspoon low-oxalate turmeric
- Salt and pepper, to taste

DIRECTIONS

1. Warm the olive oil in a big pot over medium heat.
2. Sauté the diced onion and minced garlic until aromatic and translucent in the pot.
3. Cook for a few Minutes, until the carrots and celery are slightly softened, in the pot.
4. To the pot, add the washed lentils, vegetable broth, ground cumin, ground coriander, turmeric, salt, and pepper.
5. Bring the soup to a boil, then reduce to a low heat and simmer for 1 hour, or until the lentils are cooked.
6. If required, adjust the seasonings.
7. Serve the low-oxalate lentil soup hot, garnished if desired with fresh cilantro.

NUTRITIONAL FACTS (PER SERVING)

Calories: 200
Protein: 13g
Carbohydrates: 32g
Fat: 3g

LOW-OXALATE CREAMY BROCCOLI SOUP

Serves: 4
Prep time: 10 Minutes
Total time: 30 Minutes

INGREDIENTS

- 2 cups low-oxalate broccoli florets
- 1 tablespoon low-oxalate olive oil
- 1 medium low-oxalate onion, diced
- 2 cloves low-oxalate garlic, minced
- 4 cups low-oxalate vegetable broth
- 1 cup low-oxalate almond milk or low-oxalate alternative
- Salt and pepper, to taste

DIRECTIONS

1. Broccoli florets should be steamed or blanched until soft.
2. Warm the olive oil in a big pot over medium heat.
3. Sauté the diced onion and minced garlic until aromatic and translucent in the pot.
4. Cook for a few Minutes to infuse the flavours with the steamed broccoli florets.
5. Bring the mixture to a boil with the vegetable broth.
6. Lower the heat to low and leave it to simmer for 10 Minutes.
7. Puree the soup with an immersion blender or in a blender until smooth.
8. Stir in the almond milk and return the soup to the pot.
9. Season to taste with salt and pepper.

10. Remove the soup from the heat after it has warmed through.
11. Serve the creamy broccoli soup with a drizzle of olive oil or a sprinkling of black pepper hot.

NUTRITIONAL FACTS (PER SERVING)

Calories: 100
Protein: 4g
Carbohydrates: 12g
Fat: 5g

LOW-OXALATE SPICY BLACK BEAN SOUP

Serves: 4
Prep time: 10 Minutes
Total time: 30 Minutes

INGREDIENTS

- 2 cans (15 ounces each) low-oxalate black beans, rinsed and drained
- 1 tablespoon low-oxalate olive oil
- 1 medium low-oxalate onion, diced
- 2 cloves low-oxalate garlic, minced
- 1 medium low-oxalate red bell pepper, diced
- 1 medium low-oxalate jalapeño pepper, seeds removed and diced
- 4 cups low-oxalate vegetable broth
- 1 teaspoon low-oxalate ground cumin
- 1/2 teaspoon low-oxalate chili powder
- Juice of 1 lime
- Salt and pepper, to taste

DIRECTIONS

1. Warm the olive oil in a big pot over medium heat.
2. Sauté the diced onion, minced garlic, diced red bell pepper, and diced jalapeo pepper until aromatic and translucent in the saucepan.
3. To the pot, add the black beans, vegetable broth, ground cumin, chilli powder, lime juice, salt, and pepper.
4. Bring the soup to a boil, then reduce to a low heat and leave to cook for 15-20 Minutes.
5. Puree half of the soup in a blender or with an immersion blender until smooth.
6. Return the pureed soup to the pot and mix well.

7. If required, adjust the seasonings.
8. Serve the spicy black bean soup with low-oxalate topped with fresh cilantro and a splash of lime juice hot.

NUTRITIONAL FACTS (PER SERVING)

Calories: 180
Protein: 9g
Carbohydrates: 32g
Fat: 2g

SIDE DISH RECIPES:

LOW-OXALATE GARLIC ROASTED BRUSSELS SPROUTS

Serves: 4
Prep time: 10 Minutes
Total time: 30 Minutes

INGREDIENTS

- 1 pound low-oxalate Brussels sprouts, trimmed and halved
- 2 tablespoons low-oxalate olive oil
- 3 cloves low-oxalate garlic, minced
- Salt and pepper, to taste

DIRECTIONS

1. Preheat the oven to 400°F (200°C) and line a baking sheet with parchment paper.
2. In a mixing bowl, toss the halved Brussels sprouts with olive oil, minced garlic, salt, and pepper, ensuring they are well coated.
3. Spread the Brussels sprouts in a single layer on the prepared baking sheet.
4. Roast in the preheated oven for 20-25 Minutes, or until the Brussels sprouts are tender and lightly browned, stirring halfway through.
5. Adjust the seasonings if necessary.
6. Serve the low-oxalate garlic roasted Brussels sprouts as a delicious side dish.

NUTRITIONAL FACTS (PER SERVING)

Calories: 80
Protein: 4g
Carbohydrates: 9g
Fat: 4g

LOW-OXALATE LEMON HERB ROASTED ASPARAGUS

Serves: 4
Prep time: 10 Minutes
Total time: 20 Minutes

INGREDIENTS

- 1 pound low-oxalate asparagus spears, trimmed
- 2 tablespoons low-oxalate olive oil
- Zest of 1 lemon
- 1 tablespoon low-oxalate fresh herbs (e.g., thyme, rosemary), chopped
- Salt and pepper, to taste

DIRECTIONS

1. Preheat the oven to 425 degrees Fahrenheit (220 degrees Celsius) and line a baking sheet with parchment paper.
2. Arrange the asparagus spears on the baking sheet that has been prepared.
3. Drizzle the asparagus with olive oil and season with lemon zest, chopped herbs, salt, and pepper to taste.
4. Cook for 10-12 Minutes, or until the asparagus is tender and slightly browned, in a preheated oven.
5. If required, adjust the seasonings.
6. As a tasty side dish, serve the low-oxalate lemon herb roasted asparagus.

NUTRITIONAL FACTS (PER SERVING)

Calories: 60
Protein: 2g
Carbohydrates: 5g

LOW-OXALATE QUINOA PILAF

Serves: 4
Prep time: 10 Minutes
Total time: 30 Minutes

INGREDIENTS

- 1 cup low-oxalate quinoa, rinsed
- 2 cups low-oxalate vegetable broth
- 1 tablespoon low-oxalate olive oil
- 1 medium low-oxalate onion, diced
- 2 cloves low-oxalate garlic, minced
- 1 medium low-oxalate red bell pepper, diced
- 1 medium low-oxalate yellow bell pepper, diced
- 1 teaspoon low-oxalate ground cumin
- 1/2 teaspoon low-oxalate turmeric
- Salt and pepper, to taste
- 2 tablespoons low-oxalate fresh parsley, chopped (for garnish)

DIRECTIONS

1. Combine the washed quinoa and vegetable broth in a saucepan.
2. Bring the mixture to a boil, then lower to a low heat, cover, and leave to cook for 15-20 Minutes, or until the quinoa is tender and the liquid has been absorbed.
3. Heat the olive oil in a separate big pan over medium heat.
4. Sauté the diced onion, minced garlic, diced red bell pepper, and diced yellow bell pepper until soft.
5. Pour in the cooked quinoa and toss to mix.
6. Season to taste with ground cumin, turmeric, salt, and pepper.

7. Simmer for another 2-3 Minutes to enable the flavours to blend.
8. Before serving, remove from the heat and sprinkle with chopped fresh parsley.
9. As a nutritious side dish, serve the low-oxalate quinoa pilaf.

NUTRITIONAL FACTS (PER SERVING)

Calories: 180
Protein: 6g
Carbohydrates: 30g
Fat: 4g

LOW-OXALATE ROASTED CAULIFLOWER

Serves: 4
Prep time: 10 Minutes
Total time: 30 Minutes

INGREDIENTS

- 1 medium low-oxalate cauliflower head, cut into florets
- 2 tablespoons low-oxalate olive oil
- 1 teaspoon low-oxalate ground cumin
- 1 teaspoon low-oxalate paprika
- 1/2 teaspoon low-oxalate turmeric
- Salt and pepper, to taste
- 2 tablespoons low-oxalate fresh parsley, chopped (for garnish)

DIRECTIONS

1. Preheat the oven to 425 degrees Fahrenheit (220 degrees Celsius) and line a baking sheet with parchment paper.
2. Combine the cauliflower florets, olive oil, ground cumin, paprika, turmeric, salt, and pepper in a mixing bowl and toss to coat.
3. On the prepared baking sheet, arrange the seasoned cauliflower in a single layer.
4. Cook, stirring halfway through, for 20-25 Minutes, or until the cauliflower is soft and golden brown.
5. If required, adjust the seasonings.
6. Before serving, garnish the low-oxalate roasted cauliflower with chopped fresh parsley.

NUTRITIONAL FACTS (PER SERVING)

Calories: 80
Protein: 3g
Carbohydrates: 8g
Fat: 5g

LOW-OXALATE GARLIC MASHED POTATOES

Serves: 4
Prep time: 10 Minutes
Total time: 30 Minutes

INGREDIENTS

- 4 medium low-oxalate russet potatoes, peeled and cubed
- 3 cloves low-oxalate garlic, minced
- 2 tablespoons low-oxalate butter or low-oxalate alternative
- 1/2 cup low-oxalate milk or low-oxalate alternative
- Salt and pepper, to taste
- 2 tablespoons low-oxalate fresh chives, chopped (for garnish)

DIRECTIONS

1. Cover the cubed potatoes with water in a big pot.
2. Bring the potatoes to a boil and simmer until cooked, about 15-20 Minutes.
3. Return the potatoes to the pot after draining.
4. Melt the butter in a small saucepan over low heat.
5. Sauté the minced garlic in the heated butter for a few Minutes, or until fragrant.
6. Throw in the garlic-infused butter and milk with the potatoes.
7. Mash the potatoes with a potato masher or an electric mixer until smooth and creamy.
8. Season to taste with salt and pepper.
9. Before serving, transfer the mashed potatoes to a serving dish and top with chopped fresh chives.

10. As a cosy side dish, serve the low-oxalate garlic mashed potatoes.

NUTRITIONAL FACTS (PER SERVING)

Calories: 180
Protein: 3g
Carbohydrates: 30g
Fat: 6g

LOW-OXALATE SAUTÉED SPINACH WITH GARLIC

Serves: 4
Prep time: 5 Minutes
Total time: 10 Minutes

INGREDIENTS

- 1 pound low-oxalate spinach leaves
- 2 tablespoons low-oxalate olive oil
- 3 cloves low-oxalate garlic, minced
- Salt and pepper, to taste
- Lemon wedges (optional, for serving)

DIRECTIONS

1. Thoroughly rinse and pat dry the spinach leaves.
2. Warm the olive oil in a large skillet over medium heat.
3. Sauté the minced garlic in the skillet until fragrant.
4. Working in batches if required, add the spinach leaves to the skillet.
5. Simmer for a few Minutes, stirring regularly, until the spinach is wilted and soft.
6. Season to taste with salt and pepper.
7. Take the sautéed spinach from the heat and place it in a serving dish.
8. If desired, squeeze fresh lemon juice over the spinach.
9. As a healthful side dish, serve the low-oxalate sautéed spinach with garlic.

NUTRITIONAL FACTS (PER SERVING)

Calories: 70
Protein: 4g
Carbohydrates: 4g

LOW-OXALATE ROASTED ROOT VEGETABLES

Serves: 4
Prep time: 15 Minutes
Total time: 45 Minutes

INGREDIENTS

- 2 medium low-oxalate carrots, peeled and cut into sticks
- 2 medium low-oxalate parsnips, peeled and cut into sticks
- 1 medium low-oxalate turnip, peeled and cut into sticks
- 1 medium low-oxalate beet, peeled and cut into sticks
- 1 tablespoon low-oxalate olive oil
- 1 teaspoon low-oxalate dried thyme
- Salt and pepper, to taste
- 2 tablespoons low-oxalate fresh parsley, chopped (for garnish)

DIRECTIONS

1. Preheat the oven to 425 degrees Fahrenheit (220 degrees Celsius) and line a baking sheet with parchment paper.
2. Toss the carrot, parsnip, turnip and beetroot sticks in a mixing basin with the olive oil, dried thyme, salt and pepper until completely covered.
3. On the prepared baking sheet, arrange the seasoned root vegetables in a single layer.
4. Cook for 30-35 Minutes, or until the veggies are soft and caramelised, stirring halfway through.
5. If required, adjust the seasonings.
6. Before serving, garnish the low-oxalate roasted root vegetables with chopped fresh parsley.

NUTRITIONAL FACTS (PER SERVING)

Calories: 110
Protein: 2g
Carbohydrates: 20g
Fat: 3g

STEW RECIPES:

LOW-OXALATE BEEF STEW

Serves: 6
Prep time: 20 Minutes
Total time: 2 hours 30 Minutes

INGREDIENTS

- 1.5 pounds low-oxalate beef stew meat, cubed
- 2 tablespoons low-oxalate olive oil
- 1 medium low-oxalate onion, diced
- 2 cloves low-oxalate garlic, minced
- 2 medium low-oxalate carrots, sliced
- 2 medium low-oxalate celery stalks, sliced
- 3 cups low-oxalate beef broth
- 1 cup low-oxalate diced tomatoes (canned or fresh)
- 1 teaspoon low-oxalate dried thyme
- Salt and pepper, to taste

DIRECTIONS

1. Warm the olive oil in a big pot over medium heat.
2. Brown the beef stew meat on all sides in the pot.
3. Take the beef out of the pot and set it aside.
4. Sauté the diced onion and minced garlic until aromatic and translucent in the pot.
5. Cook for a few Minutes, until the carrots and celery are slightly softened, in the pot.
6. Pour the beef broth and diced tomatoes into the pot with the beef.
7. Season with salt and pepper to taste after adding the dry thyme.

8. Bring the stew to a boil, then lower to a low heat and cover for 2 hours, or until the beef is cooked.
9. If required, adjust the seasonings.
10. Serve the low-oxalate beef stew hot, garnished if preferred with fresh parsley.

NUTRITIONAL FACTS (PER SERVING)

Calories: 300
Protein: 25g
Carbohydrates: 10g
Fat: 15g

LOW-OXALATE CHICKEN AND VEGETABLE STEW

Serves: 6
Prep time: 20 Minutes
Total time: 1 hour 30 Minutes

INGREDIENTS

- 1.5 pounds low-oxalate boneless, skinless chicken breasts, cubed
- 2 tablespoons low-oxalate olive oil
- 1 medium low-oxalate onion, diced
- 2 cloves low-oxalate garlic, minced
- 2 medium low-oxalate carrots, sliced
- 2 medium low-oxalate celery stalks, sliced
- 4 cups low-oxalate chicken broth
- 1 cup low-oxalate diced tomatoes (canned or fresh)
- 1 teaspoon low-oxalate dried thyme
- Salt and pepper, to taste

DIRECTIONS

1. Warm the olive oil in a big pot over medium heat.
2. Cook until the chicken cubes are browned on all sides in the pot.
3. Take the chicken out of the pot and set it aside.
4. Sauté the diced onion and minced garlic until aromatic and translucent in the pot.
5. Cook for a few Minutes, until the carrots and celery are slightly softened, in the pot.
6. Pour the chicken stock and diced tomatoes into the pot with the chicken.

7. Season with salt and pepper to taste after adding the dry thyme.
8. Bring the stew to a boil, then lower to a low heat and cover for 1 hour, or until the chicken is cooked through.
9. If required, adjust the seasonings.
10. Serve the low-oxalate chicken and vegetable stew hot, garnished if preferred with fresh parsley.

NUTRITIONAL FACTS (PER SERVING)

Calories: 250
Protein: 30g
Carbohydrates: 10g
Fat: 10g

LOW-OXALATE LENTIL AND VEGETABLE STEW

Serves: 6
Prep time: 15 Minutes
Total time: 1 hour 30 Minutes

INGREDIENTS

- 1 cup low-oxalate green or brown lentils, rinsed and drained
- 2 tablespoons low-oxalate olive oil
- 1 medium low-oxalate onion, diced
- 2 cloves low-oxalate garlic, minced
- 2 medium low-oxalate carrots, sliced
- 2 medium low-oxalate celery stalks, sliced
- 4 cups low-oxalate vegetable broth
- 1 cup low-oxalate diced tomatoes (canned or fresh)
- 1 teaspoon low-oxalate dried thyme
- Salt and pepper, to taste

DIRECTIONS

1. Warm the olive oil in a big pot over medium heat.
2. Sauté the diced onion and minced garlic until aromatic and translucent in the pot.
3. Cook for a few Minutes, until the carrots and celery are slightly softened, in the pot.
4. To the pot, add the rinsed lentils, vegetable broth, diced tomatoes, dried thyme, salt, and pepper.
5. Bring the stew to a boil, then lower to a low heat and cover for 1 hour, or until the lentils are cooked.
6. If required, adjust the seasonings.
7. Serve the low-oxalate lentil and vegetable stew hot, garnished if preferred with fresh parsley.

NUTRITIONAL FACTS (PER SERVING)

Calories: 200
Protein: 10g
Carbohydrates: 30g
Fat: 5g

LOW-OXALATE MUSHROOM AND BARLEY STEW

Serves: 6
Prep time: 15 Minutes
Total time: 1 hour 30 Minutes

INGREDIENTS

- 1 cup low-oxalate pearl barley
- 2 tablespoons low-oxalate olive oil
- 1 medium low-oxalate onion, diced
- 2 cloves low-oxalate garlic, minced
- 8 ounces low-oxalate mushrooms, sliced
- 2 medium low-oxalate carrots, sliced
- 2 medium low-oxalate celery stalks, sliced
- 4 cups low-oxalate vegetable broth
- 1 teaspoon low-oxalate dried thyme
- Salt and pepper, to taste

DIRECTIONS

1. Combine the pearl barley and 2 cups of water in a saucepan.
2. Bring the mixture to a boil, then reduce to a low heat, cover, and continue to cook for 45 Minutes, or until the barley is soft and the water has been absorbed.
3. Warm the olive oil in a big pot over medium heat.
4. Sauté the diced onion and minced garlic until aromatic and translucent in the pot.
5. Cook for a few Minutes, until the mushrooms, carrots, and celery are slightly softened, in the saucepan.
6. To the pot, add the cooked barley, vegetable broth, dried thyme, salt, and pepper.

7. Bring the stew to a boil, then lower to a low heat and cover for 30 Minutes to allow the flavours to combine.
8. If required, adjust the seasonings.
9. Serve the low-oxalate mushroom and barley stew hot, garnished if preferred with fresh parsley.

NUTRITIONAL FACTS (PER SERVING)

Calories: 220
Protein: 6g
Carbohydrates: 40g
Fat: 5g

LOW-OXALATE WHITE BEAN AND VEGETABLE STEW

Serves: 6
Prep time: 20 Minutes
Total time: 1 hour 30 Minutes

INGREDIENTS

- 2 cups low-oxalate cooked white beans (canned or cooked from dried beans)
- 2 tablespoons low-oxalate olive oil
- 1 medium low-oxalate onion, diced
- 2 cloves low-oxalate garlic, minced
- 2 medium low-oxalate carrots, sliced
- 2 medium low-oxalate celery stalks, sliced
- 4 cups low-oxalate vegetable broth
- 1 cup low-oxalate diced tomatoes (canned or fresh)
- 1 teaspoon low-oxalate dried thyme
- Salt and pepper, to taste

DIRECTIONS

1. Warm the olive oil in a big pot over medium heat.
2. Sauté the diced onion and minced garlic until aromatic and translucent in the pot.
3. Cook for a few Minutes, until the carrots and celery are slightly softened, in the pot.
4. To the pot, add the cooked white beans, vegetable broth, diced tomatoes, dried thyme, salt, and pepper.
5. Bring the stew to a boil, then lower to a low heat and cover for 1 hour, or until the veggies are cooked.
6. If required, adjust the seasonings.

7. Serve the low-oxalate white bean and vegetable stew hot, garnished if preferred with fresh parsley.

NUTRITIONAL FACTS (PER SERVING)

Calories: 180
Protein: 8g
Carbohydrates: 30g
Fat: 5g

LOW-OXALATE LENTIL AND SPINACH STEW

Serves: 6
Prep time: 15 Minutes
Total time: 1 hour 15 Minutes

INGREDIENTS

- 1 cup low-oxalate green or brown lentils, rinsed and drained
- 2 tablespoons low-oxalate olive oil
- 1 medium low-oxalate onion, diced
- 2 cloves low-oxalate garlic, minced
- 4 cups low-oxalate vegetable broth
- 1 can (14 ounces) low-oxalate diced tomatoes
- 2 cups low-oxalate fresh spinach leaves
- 1 teaspoon low-oxalate dried thyme
- Salt and pepper, to taste

DIRECTIONS

1. Warm the olive oil in a big pot over medium heat.
2. Sauté the diced onion and minced garlic until aromatic and translucent in the pot.
3. To the pot, add the rinsed lentils, vegetable broth, chopped tomatoes (including juice), dried thyme, salt, and pepper.
4. Bring the stew to a boil, then lower to a low heat and cover for 1 hour, or until the lentils are cooked.
5. Let the fresh spinach leaves to wilt in the stew for a few Minutes.
6. If required, adjust the seasonings.
7. Serve the low-oxalate lentil and spinach stew hot, garnished if preferred with fresh parsley.

NUTRITIONAL FACTS (PER SERVING)

Calories: 200
Protein: 10g
Carbohydrates: 30g
Fat: 5g

LOW-OXALATE VEGETABLE AND QUINOA STEW

Serves: 6
Prep time: 15 Minutes
Total time: 45 Minutes

INGREDIENTS

- 1 cup low-oxalate quinoa, rinsed and drained
- 2 tablespoons low-oxalate olive oil
- 1 medium low-oxalate onion, diced
- 2 cloves low-oxalate garlic, minced
- 2 medium low-oxalate carrots, sliced
- 2 medium low-oxalate celery stalks, sliced
- 4 cups low-oxalate vegetable broth
- 1 cup low-oxalate diced tomatoes (canned or fresh)
- 1 teaspoon low-oxalate dried thyme
- Salt and pepper, to taste

DIRECTIONS

1. Combine the washed quinoa and 2 cups of water in a saucepan.
2. Bring the mixture to a boil, then lower to a low heat, cover, and leave to cook for 15 Minutes, or until the quinoa is tender and the water has been absorbed.
3. Warm the olive oil in a big pot over medium heat.
4. Sauté the diced onion and minced garlic until aromatic and translucent in the pot.
5. Cook for a few Minutes, until the carrots and celery are slightly softened, in the pot.
6. To the pot, add the cooked quinoa, vegetable broth, diced tomatoes, dried thyme, salt, and pepper.

7. Bring the stew to a boil, then reduce to a low heat and cover it for 15-20 Minutes to allow the flavours to blend.
8. If required, adjust the seasonings.
9. Serve the low-oxalate vegetable and quinoa stew hot, garnished if preferred with fresh parsley.

NUTRITIONAL FACTS (PER SERVING)

Calories: 200
Protein: 6g
Carbohydrates: 30g
Fat: 6g

CASSEROLE RECIPES:

LOW-OXALATE CHICKEN AND VEGETABLE CASSEROLE

Serves: 6
Prep time: 15 Minutes
Total time: 1 hour 15 Minutes

INGREDIENTS

- 1.5 pounds low-oxalate boneless, skinless chicken breasts, cubed
- 2 tablespoons low-oxalate olive oil
- 1 medium low-oxalate onion, diced
- 2 cloves low-oxalate garlic, minced
- 2 medium low-oxalate carrots, sliced
- 2 medium low-oxalate zucchini, sliced
- 1 medium low-oxalate bell pepper, diced
- 1 cup low-oxalate cherry tomatoes, halved
- 1 cup low-oxalate chicken broth
- 1 teaspoon low-oxalate dried thyme
- 1 teaspoon low-oxalate dried oregano
- Salt and pepper, to taste

DIRECTIONS

1. Preheat the oven to 375°F (190°C) and coat a baking dish with cooking spray.
2. Warm the olive oil in a large skillet over medium heat.
3. Cook until the onion and garlic are aromatic and transparent in the skillet.
4. Cook until the cubed chicken is browned on all sides in the skillet.

5. Remove from the fire and add the sliced carrots, zucchini, diced bell pepper, and cherry tomatoes.
6. Whisk together the chicken broth, dried thyme, dried oregano, salt, and pepper in a small basin.
7. Stir in the broth mixture over the chicken and veggies in the skillet.
8. Cover with foil the mixture in the oiled baking dish.
9. Bake for 45-50 Minutes, or until the chicken is cooked through and the vegetables are soft, in a preheated oven.
10. Remove the foil and continue to broil for another 2-3 Minutes to lightly brown the top.
11. If required, adjust the seasonings.
12. Serve the low-oxalate chicken and vegetable dish at room temperature.

NUTRITIONAL FACTS (PER SERVING)

Calories: 250
Protein: 30g
Carbohydrates: 10g
Fat: 10g

LOW-OXALATE CAULIFLOWER AND BROCCOLI CASSEROLE

Serves: 6
Prep time: 20 Minutes
Total time: 1 hour

INGREDIENTS

- 1 medium low-oxalate cauliflower, cut into florets
- 1 medium low-oxalate broccoli, cut into florets
- 2 tablespoons low-oxalate olive oil
- 2 cloves low-oxalate garlic, minced
- 1 cup low-oxalate shredded cheddar cheese
- 1/2 cup low-oxalate grated Parmesan cheese
- 1 cup low-oxalate plain Greek yogurt
- 1/2 cup low-oxalate breadcrumbs
- Salt and pepper, to taste

DIRECTIONS

1. Preheat the oven to 375°F (190°C) and coat a baking dish with cooking spray.
2. The cauliflower and broccoli florets should be steamed until soft, then drained properly.
3. Warm the olive oil in a large skillet over medium heat.
4. Sauté the minced garlic in the skillet until fragrant.
5. Take the skillet off the heat and add the cooked cauliflower and broccoli.
6. Combine the shredded cheddar cheese, grated Parmesan cheese, Greek yoghurt, salt, and pepper in a separate bowl.
7. Stir the cheese mixture into the skillet with the vegetables until evenly coated.
8. Spread the breadcrumbs equally over the top of the mixture in the greased baking dish.

9. Bake for 30-35 Minutes, or until the casserole is heated through and the breadcrumbs are golden brown, in a preheated oven.
10. If required, adjust the seasonings.
11. Serve the cauliflower and broccoli casserole warm.

NUTRITIONAL FACTS (PER SERVING)

Calories: 200
Protein: 15g
Carbohydrates: 10g
Fat: 12g

LOW-OXALATE QUINOA AND VEGETABLE CASSEROLE

Serves: 6
Prep time: 20 Minutes
Total time: 1 hour

INGREDIENTS

- 1 cup low-oxalate quinoa, rinsed and drained
- 2 cups low-oxalate vegetable broth
- 2 tablespoons low-oxalate olive oil
- 1 medium low-oxalate onion, diced
- 2 cloves low-oxalate garlic, minced
- 1 medium low-oxalate bell pepper, diced
- 2 medium low-oxalate zucchini, sliced
- 1 cup low-oxalate diced tomatoes (canned or fresh)
- 1 cup low-oxalate shredded mozzarella cheese
- 1/4 cup low-oxalate grated Parmesan cheese
- 1 teaspoon low-oxalate dried basil
- Salt and pepper, to taste

DIRECTIONS

1. Preheat the oven to 375°F (190°C) and coat a baking dish with cooking spray.
2. The cauliflower and broccoli florets should be steamed until soft, then drained properly.
3. Warm the olive oil in a large skillet over medium heat.
4. Sauté the minced garlic in the skillet until fragrant.
5. Take the skillet off the heat and add the cooked cauliflower and broccoli.
6. Combine the shredded cheddar cheese, grated Parmesan cheese, Greek yoghurt, salt, and pepper in a separate bowl.

7. Stir the cheese mixture into the skillet with the vegetables until evenly coated.
8. Spread the breadcrumbs equally over the top of the mixture in the greased baking dish.
9. Bake for 30-35 Minutes, or until the casserole is heated through and the breadcrumbs are golden brown, in a preheated oven.
10. If required, adjust the seasonings.
11. Serve the cauliflower and broccoli casserole warm.

NUTRITIONAL FACTS (PER SERVING)

Calories: 220
Protein: 10g
Carbohydrates: 30g
Fat: 8g

LOW-OXALATE EGGPLANT AND TOMATO CASSEROLE

Serves: 6
Prep time: 30 Minutes
Total time: 1 hour 30 Minutes

INGREDIENTS

- 2 medium low-oxalate eggplants, sliced into rounds
- 2 tablespoons low-oxalate olive oil
- 1 medium low-oxalate onion, diced
- 2 cloves low-oxalate garlic, minced
- 1 can (14 ounces) low-oxalate diced tomatoes
- 1/4 cup low-oxalate tomato paste
- 1 teaspoon low-oxalate dried oregano
- 1/2 teaspoon low-oxalate dried basil
- Salt and pepper, to taste
- 1 cup low-oxalate shredded mozzarella cheese
- 1/4 cup low-oxalate grated Parmesan cheese
- Fresh basil leaves (for garnish)

DIRECTIONS

1. Preheat the oven to 375°F (190°C) and coat a baking dish with cooking spray.
2. Brush both sides of the aubergine slices with olive oil and place them on a baking pan.
3. Bake the eggplant slices for 20-25 Minutes, or until soft and gently browned in a preheated oven.
4. Warm the olive oil in a large skillet over medium heat.
5. Cook until the onion and garlic are aromatic and transparent in the skillet.

6. Combine the diced tomatoes, tomato paste, dried oregano, dry basil, salt, and pepper in a mixing bowl.
7. Let the tomato sauce to simmer for 10-15 Minutes to enable the flavours to blend.
8. Layer half of the aubergine slices in the prepared baking dish, followed by half of the tomato sauce.
9. Layer the leftover eggplant and tomato sauce on top.
10. Top with the shredded mozzarella and grated Parmesan cheese.
11. Bake for 30 Minutes, or until the casserole is thoroughly heated and the cheese is melted and bubbling.
12. Before serving, garnish the low-oxalate aubergine and tomato stew with fresh basil leaves.

NUTRITIONAL FACTS (PER SERVING)

Calories: 180
Protein: 8g
Carbohydrates: 15g
Fat: 10g

LOW-OXALATE SPINACH AND ARTICHOKE CASSEROLE

Serves: 6
Prep time: 20 Minutes
Total time: 45 Minutes

INGREDIENTS

- 2 cups low-oxalate frozen chopped spinach, thawed and drained
- 1 can (14 ounces) low-oxalate artichoke hearts, drained and chopped
- 1 cup low-oxalate sour cream
- 1 cup low-oxalate mayonnaise
- 1/2 cup low-oxalate grated Parmesan cheese
- 1/2 cup low-oxalate shredded mozzarella cheese
- 2 cloves low-oxalate garlic, minced
- Salt and pepper, to taste

DIRECTIONS

1. Preheat the oven to 375°F (190°C) and grease a baking dish.
2. In a large bowl, combine the chopped spinach, chopped artichoke hearts, sour cream, mayonnaise, grated Parmesan cheese, shredded mozzarella cheese, minced garlic, salt, and pepper.
3. Stir the mixture until well combined.
4. Transfer the mixture to the greased baking dish and spread it evenly.
5. Bake in the preheated oven for 25-30 Minutes, or until the casserole is heated through and the top is golden brown and bubbly.
6. Adjust the seasonings if necessary.

7. Serve the low-oxalate spinach and artichoke casserole hot.

NUTRITIONAL FACTS (PER SERVING)

Calories: 250
Protein: 10g
Carbohydrates: 10g
Fat: 20g

LOW-OXALATE LENTIL AND MUSHROOM CASSEROLE

Serves: 6
Prep time: 20 Minutes
Total time: 1 hour

INGREDIENTS

- 1 cup low-oxalate green or brown lentils, rinsed and drained
- 2 cups low-oxalate vegetable broth
- 2 tablespoons low-oxalate olive oil
- 1 medium low-oxalate onion, diced
- 8 ounces low-oxalate mushrooms, sliced
- 2 cloves low-oxalate garlic, minced
- 1 teaspoon low-oxalate dried thyme
- 1/2 teaspoon low-oxalate dried rosemary
- Salt and pepper, to taste
- 1 cup low-oxalate shredded mozzarella cheese
- 1/4 cup low-oxalate grated Parmesan cheese

DIRECTIONS

Preheat the oven to 375°F (190°C) and grease a baking dish.

In a saucepan, bring the vegetable broth to a boil, then add the rinsed lentils.

Reduce the heat to low, cover, and simmer for 20-25 Minutes, or until the lentils are tender and the liquid is absorbed.

In a large skillet, heat the olive oil over medium heat.

Add the diced onion, sliced mushrooms, and minced garlic to the skillet and sauté until the mushrooms are golden brown and tender.

Stir in the cooked lentils, dried thyme, dried rosemary, salt, and pepper.

Transfer the mixture to the greased baking dish and spread it evenly.

Sprinkle the shredded mozzarella and grated Parmesan cheese over the top.

Bake in the preheated oven for 20-25 Minutes, or until the casserole is heated through and the cheese is melted and bubbly.

Adjust the seasonings if necessary.

NUTRITIONAL FACTS (PER SERVING)

Calories: 220
Protein: 12g
Carbohydrates: 25g
Fat: 10g

PIZZA RECIPES:

LOW-OXALATE MARGHERITA PIZZA

Serves: 2
Prep time: 15 Minutes
Total time: 30 Minutes

INGREDIENTS

- 1 low-oxalate pizza crust (store-bought or homemade)
- 1/2 cup low-oxalate pizza sauce
- 1 cup low-oxalate shredded mozzarella cheese
- 2 medium low-oxalate tomatoes, sliced
- Fresh basil leaves, for garnish
- Salt and pepper, to taste

DIRECTIONS

1. Preheat the oven to the temperature specified on the pizza crust package or recipe.
2. Place the pizza crust on a baking sheet or pizza stone.
3. Spread the pizza sauce evenly over the crust.
4. Sprinkle the shredded mozzarella cheese over the sauce.
5. Arrange the tomato slices on top of the cheese.
6. Season with salt and pepper to taste.
7. Bake in the preheated oven according to the crust instructions, usually around 12-15 Minutes or until the cheese is melted and bubbly.
8. Remove from the oven and garnish with fresh basil leaves.
9. Slice and serve the low-oxalate Margherita pizza hot.

NUTRITIONAL FACTS (PER SERVING)

Calories: 300
Protein: 15g
Carbohydrates: 30g
Fat: 12g

LOW-OXALATE MEDITERRANEAN VEGGIE PIZZA

Serves: 2
Prep time: 20 Minutes
Total time: 35 Minutes

INGREDIENTS

- 1 low-oxalate pizza crust (store-bought or homemade)
- 1/4 cup low-oxalate tomato paste
- 1 teaspoon low-oxalate dried oregano
- 1/2 teaspoon low-oxalate dried basil
- 1/4 teaspoon low-oxalate garlic powder
- 1/2 cup low-oxalate shredded mozzarella cheese
- 1/4 cup low-oxalate crumbled feta cheese
- 1/4 cup low-oxalate sliced black olives
- 1/4 cup low-oxalate sliced red onions
- 1/4 cup low-oxalate sliced roasted red peppers
- 2 tablespoons low-oxalate chopped fresh parsley

DIRECTIONS

1. Preheat the oven according to the instructions on the pizza crust package or recipe.
2. Put the pizza crust on a pizza stone or baking sheet.
3. Combine the tomato paste, dried oregano, dried basil, and garlic powder in a small bowl.
4. Evenly distribute the tomato paste mixture over the crust.
5. Over the sauce, scatter the shredded mozzarella cheese.
6. Crumbled feta cheese, black olives, red onions, and roasted red peppers go on top.

7. Bake in a preheated oven for 12-15 Minutes, or until the cheese is melted and bubbling, according to the crust
8. Remove from the oven and sprinkle with fresh parsley.

NUTRITIONAL FACTS (PER SERVING)

Calories: 280
Protein: 15g
Carbohydrates: 30g
Fat: 10g

LOW-OXALATE BBQ CHICKEN PIZZA

Serves: 2
Prep time: 15 Minutes
Total time: 30 Minutes

INGREDIENTS

- 1 low-oxalate pizza crust (store-bought or homemade)
- 1/4 cup low-oxalate barbecue sauce
- 1 cup low-oxalate shredded mozzarella cheese
- 1/2 cup low-oxalate cooked chicken breast, shredded
- 1/4 cup low-oxalate sliced red onions
- 1/4 cup low-oxalate chopped fresh cilantro

DIRECTIONS

1. Preheat the oven to the temperature specified on the pizza crust package or recipe.
2. Place the pizza crust on a baking sheet or pizza stone.
3. Spread the barbecue sauce evenly over the crust.
4. Sprinkle the shredded mozzarella cheese over the sauce.
5. Top with shredded chicken breast and sliced red onions.
6. Bake in the preheated oven according to the crust instructions, usually around 12-15 Minutes or until the cheese is melted and bubbly.
7. Remove from the oven and garnish with chopped fresh cilantro.
8. Slice and serve the low-oxalate BBQ chicken pizza hot.

NUTRITIONAL FACTS (PER SERVING)

Calories: 320
Protein: 20g
Carbohydrates: 30g

LOW-OXALATE PESTO AND TOMATO PIZZA

Serves: 2
Prep time: 15 Minutes
Total time: 30 Minutes

INGREDIENTS

- 1 low-oxalate pizza crust (store-bought or homemade)
- 1/4 cup low-oxalate pesto sauce
- 1 cup low-oxalate shredded mozzarella cheese
- 1 cup low-oxalate cherry tomatoes, halved
- Fresh basil leaves, for garnish
- Salt and pepper, to taste

DIRECTIONS

1. Preheat the oven according to the instructions on the pizza crust package or recipe.
2. Put the pizza crust on a pizza stone or baking sheet.
3. Evenly distribute the pesto sauce over the dough.
4. Over the sauce, scatter the shredded mozzarella cheese.
5. Place the cherry tomato halves atop the cheese.
6. Season to taste with salt and pepper.
7. Bake in a preheated oven for 12-15 Minutes, or until the cheese is melted and bubbling, according to the crust DIRECTIONS.
8. Remove from the oven and sprinkle with fresh basil leaves to serve.
9. Slice the low-oxalate pesto and tomato pizza and serve it hot.

NUTRITIONAL FACTS (PER SERVING)

Calories: 280
Protein: 15g
Carbohydrates: 30g
Fat: 10g

LOW-OXALATE GREEK PIZZA

Serves: 2
Prep time: 20 Minutes
Total time: 35 Minutes

INGREDIENTS

- 1 low-oxalate pizza crust (store-bought or homemade)
- 1/4 cup low-oxalate tomato sauce
- 1 cup low-oxalate shredded mozzarella cheese
- 1/4 cup low-oxalate crumbled feta cheese
- 1/4 cup low-oxalate sliced black olives
- 1/4 cup low-oxalate sliced red onions
- 1/4 cup low-oxalate diced tomatoes
- 2 tablespoons low-oxalate chopped fresh oregano

DIRECTIONS

1. Preheat the oven according to the instructions on the pizza crust package or recipe.
2. Put the pizza crust on a pizza stone or baking sheet.
3. Evenly distribute the tomato sauce over the crust.
4. Over the sauce, scatter the shredded mozzarella cheese.
5. Crumbled feta cheese, black olives, sliced red onions, and chopped tomatoes go on top.
6. Bake in a preheated oven for 12-15 Minutes, or until the cheese is melted and bubbling, according to the crust DIRECTIONS.
7. Remove from the oven and sprinkle with fresh oregano.
8. Slice the low-oxalate Greek pizza and serve it hot.

NUTRITIONAL FACTS (PER SERVING)

Calories: 280
Protein: 15g
Carbohydrates: 30g
Fat: 10g

LOW-OXALATE VEGGIE SUPREME PIZZA

Serves: 2
Prep time: 20 Minutes
Total time: 35 Minutes

INGREDIENTS

- 1 low-oxalate pizza crust (store-bought or homemade)
- 1/4 cup low-oxalate tomato sauce
- 1 cup low-oxalate shredded mozzarella cheese
- 1/4 cup low-oxalate sliced mushrooms
- 1/4 cup low-oxalate sliced bell peppers
- 1/4 cup low-oxalate sliced red onions
- 1/4 cup low-oxalate sliced black olives
- 1/4 cup low-oxalate diced tomatoes
- 1/2 teaspoon low-oxalate dried oregano
- 1/2 teaspoon low-oxalate dried basil
- Salt and pepper, to taste

DIRECTIONS

1. Preheat the oven according to the instructions on the pizza crust package or recipe.
2. Put the pizza crust on a pizza stone or baking sheet.
3. Evenly distribute the tomato sauce over the crust.
4. Over the sauce, scatter the shredded mozzarella cheese.
5. Add sliced mushrooms, bell peppers, red onions, black olives, and chopped tomatoes to the top.
6. Sprinkle the toppings with the dried oregano and basil.
7. Season to taste with salt and pepper.
8. Bake in a preheated oven for 12-15 Minutes, or until the cheese is melted and bubbling, according to the crust

NUTRITIONAL FACTS (PER SERVING)
Calories: 270
Protein: 15g
Carbohydrates: 30g
Fat: 10g

LOW-OXALATE WHITE PIZZA WITH SPINACH AND GARLIC

Serves: 2
Prep time: 20 Minutes
Total time: 35 Minutes

INGREDIENTS

- 1 low-oxalate pizza crust (store-bought or homemade)
- 1/4 cup low-oxalate olive oil
- 2 cloves low-oxalate garlic, minced
- 1 cup low-oxalate shredded mozzarella cheese
- 1 cup low-oxalate shredded fontina cheese
- 2 cups low-oxalate fresh spinach leaves
- Salt and pepper, to taste

DIRECTIONS

1. Preheat the oven to the temperature specified on the pizza crust package or recipe.
2. Place the pizza crust on a baking sheet or pizza stone.
3. In a small bowl, mix together the olive oil and minced garlic.
4. Brush the garlic-infused oil over the crust.
5. Sprinkle the shredded mozzarella cheese and shredded fontina cheese over the crust.
6. Top with fresh spinach leaves.
7. Season with salt and pepper to taste.
8. Bake in the preheated oven according to the crust instructions, usually around 12-15 Minutes or until the cheese is melted and bubbly.
9. Slice and serve the low-oxalate white pizza with spinach and garlic hot.

NUTRITIONAL FACTS (PER SERVING)

Calories: 290
Protein: 15g
Carbohydrates: 30g
Fat: 12g

BOOK 2

40+Salad, Side dishes and pasta recipes for a healthy and balanced Low oxalate diet

SIDE DISH RECIPES

STEAMED BROCCOLI WITH LEMON GARLIC SAUCE

Serves: 4
Prep time: 10 Minutes
Total time: 15 Minutes

INGREDIENTS

- 4 cups broccoli florets
- 2 tablespoons olive oil
- 2 cloves garlic, minced
- 1 tablespoon lemon juice
- Salt and pepper to taste

DIRECTIONS

1. Cook the broccoli for 5-7 Minutes, or until soft.
2. In a small saucepan, heat olive oil over medium heat.
3. Sauté the minced garlic for 1-2 Minutes, or until fragrant.
4. Remove from the fire and add the lemon juice.
5. Sprinkle the steaming broccoli with the lemon garlic sauce.
6. Season with salt and pepper to taste.
7. Serve immediately.

NUTRITIONAL FACTS (PER SERVING)

Approximately 80 calories, 2g protein, 6g fat, 6g carbohydrates

ROASTED ASPARAGUS WITH PARMESAN CHEESE

Serves: 4
Prep time: 10 Minutes
Total time: 20 Minutes

INGREDIENTS

- 1 bunch asparagus, trimmed
- 2 tablespoons olive oil
- 2 tablespoons grated Parmesan cheese
- Salt and pepper to taste

DIRECTIONS

1. Preheat the oven to 425°F (220°C).
2. Place the trimmed asparagus on a baking sheet.
3. Drizzle with olive oil and sprinkle with Parmesan cheese.
4. Season with salt and pepper.
5. Roast for 12-15 Minutes until the asparagus is tender and slightly crispy.
6. Serve hot.

NUTRITIONAL FACTS (PER SERVING)

Approximately 70 calories, 4g protein, 5g fat, 4g carbohydrates

CUCUMBER TOMATO SALAD

Serves: 4
Prep time: 10 Minutes
Total time: 10 Minutes

INGREDIENTS

- 2 medium cucumbers, sliced
- 2 medium tomatoes, chopped
- 1/4 red onion, thinly sliced
- 2 tablespoons chopped fresh dill
- 2 tablespoons olive oil
- 1 tablespoon apple cider vinegar
- Salt and pepper to taste

DIRECTIONS

1. Combine sliced cucumbers, chopped tomatoes, thinly sliced red onion, and chopped fresh dill in a large mixing dish.
2. Drizzle with apple cider vinegar and olive oil.
3. Season with salt and pepper to taste.
4. Gently toss all INGREDIENTS together.
5. Chill before serving.

NUTRITIONAL FACTS (PER SERVING)

Approximately 60 calories, 1g protein, 5g fat, 4g carbohydrates

OVEN-ROASTED BRUSSELS SPROUTS

Serves: 4
Prep time: 10 Minutes
Total time: 30 Minutes

INGREDIENTS

- 1 pound Brussels sprouts, trimmed and halved
- 2 tablespoons olive oil
- Salt and pepper to taste

DIRECTIONS

1. Preheat the oven to 425°F (220°C).
2. Place the trimmed and halved Brussels sprouts on a baking sheet.
3. Drizzle with olive oil and season with salt and pepper.
4. Toss to coat the Brussels sprouts evenly.
5. Roast for 20-25 Minutes, stirring halfway through, until the Brussels sprouts are tender and lightly browned.
6. Serve hot.

NUTRITIONAL FACTS (PER SERVING)

Approximately 70 calories, 4g protein, 4g fat, 8g carbohydrates

GRILLED ZUCCHINI WITH HERBS

Serves: 4
Prep time: 10 Minutes
Total time: 15 Minutes

INGREDIENTS

- 2 medium zucchini, sliced lengthwise
- 2 tablespoons olive oil
- 1 tablespoon chopped fresh herbs (such as basil, thyme, or oregano)
- Salt and pepper to taste

DIRECTIONS

1. Preheat the grill to medium heat.
2. Brush both sides of the zucchini slices with olive oil.
3. Sprinkle with chopped fresh herbs, salt, and pepper.
4. Place the zucchini slices on the grill and cook for 3-4 Minutes per side until tender and grill marks appear.
5. Remove from the grill and let cool slightly before serving.

NUTRITIONAL FACTS (PER SERVING)

Approximately 60 calories, 2g protein, 5g fat, 3g carbohydrates

CAULIFLOWER RICE PILAF

Serves: 4
Prep time: 10 Minutes
Total time: 20 Minutes

INGREDIENTS

- 1 head cauliflower, riced
- 1 tablespoon olive oil
- 1/4 cup diced onion
- 1/4 cup diced bell pepper
- 1/4 cup diced carrot
- 1/4 cup peas
- 2 cloves garlic, minced
- 1 teaspoon turmeric
- Salt and pepper to taste
- Chopped fresh parsley for garnish

DIRECTIONS

1. Warm the olive oil in a large skillet over medium heat.
2. Diced onion, bell pepper, carrot, peas, and minced garlic are all good additions.
3. Sauté for 3-4 Minutes, or until the vegetables have softened slightly.
4. In the skillet, combine the riced cauliflower and turmeric.
5. Season with salt and pepper to taste.
6. Sauté, stirring regularly, for 5-6 Minutes, or until the cauliflower is cooked through and soft.
7. Before serving, remove from the heat and garnish with chopped fresh parsley.

NUTRITIONAL FACTS (PER SERVING)

Approximately 60 calories, 3g protein, 3g fat, 8g carbohydrates

ROASTED GARLIC MUSHROOMS

Serves: 4
Prep time: 10 Minutes
Total time: 30 Minutes

INGREDIENTS

- 1 pound mushrooms, cleaned and quartered
- 2 tablespoons olive oil
- 4 cloves garlic, minced
- 1 tablespoon chopped fresh thyme
- Salt and pepper to taste

DIRECTIONS

1. Preheat the oven to 425°F (220°C).
2. In a mixing bowl, combine quartered mushrooms, olive oil, minced garlic, chopped fresh thyme, salt, and pepper.
3. Toss to coat the mushrooms evenly.
4. Spread the mushrooms in a single layer on a baking sheet.
5. Roast for 20-25 Minutes, stirring halfway through, until the mushrooms are tender and golden brown.
6. Serve hot.

NUTRITIONAL FACTS (PER SERVING)

Approximately 70 calories, 4g protein, 4g fat, 6g carbohydrates

BAKED SWEET POTATO FRIES

Serves: 4
Prep time: 10 Minutes
Total time: 30 Minutes

INGREDIENTS

- 2 medium sweet potatoes, cut into fries
- 2 tablespoons olive oil
- 1 teaspoon paprika
- 1/2 teaspoon garlic powder
- 1/2 teaspoon onion powder
- Salt and pepper to taste

DIRECTIONS

1. Preheat the oven to 425°F (220°C).
2. In a large bowl, combine sweet potato fries, olive oil, paprika, garlic powder, onion powder, salt, and pepper.
3. Toss to coat the fries evenly with the seasonings.
4. Spread the fries in a single layer on a baking sheet.
5. Bake for 20-25 Minutes, flipping once halfway through, until the fries are crispy and golden brown.
6. Serve hot.

NUTRITIONAL FACTS (PER SERVING)

Approximately 100 calories, 2g protein, 5g fat, 15g carbohydrates

ROASTED CARROTS WITH CUMIN

Serves: 4
Prep time: 10 Minutes
Total time: 25 Minutes

INGREDIENTS

- 1 pound baby carrots
- 2 tablespoons olive oil
- 1 teaspoon ground cumin
- 1/2 teaspoon paprika
- Salt and pepper to taste
- Chopped fresh parsley for garnish

DIRECTIONS

1. Preheat the oven to 425°F (220°C).
2. In a mixing bowl, combine baby carrots, olive oil, ground cumin, paprika, salt, and pepper.
3. Toss to coat the carrots evenly with the seasonings.
4. Spread the carrots in a single layer on a baking sheet.
5. Roast for 15-20 Minutes, stirring once halfway through, until the carrots are tender and caramelized.
6. Remove from the oven and garnish with chopped fresh parsley before serving.

NUTRITIONAL FACTS (PER SERVING)

Approximately 70 calories, 1g protein, 5g fat, 7g carbohydrates

GRILLED EGGPLANT WITH YOGURT SAUCE

Serves: 4
Prep time: 15 Minutes
Total time: 25 Minutes

INGREDIENTS

- 1 large eggplant, sliced into rounds
- 2 tablespoons olive oil
- 1/2 teaspoon ground cumin
- 1/2 teaspoon paprika
- Salt and pepper to taste
- 1/2 cup Greek yogurt
- 1 clove garlic, minced
- 1 tablespoon chopped fresh mint
- Lemon wedges for serving

DIRECTIONS

1. Heat the grill to medium-high.
2. Brush the eggplant slices with olive oil on both sides.
3. Season with cumin, paprika, salt, and pepper.
4. Grill the eggplant slices for 3-4 Minutes per side until soft and grill marks form.
5. Combine Greek yoghurt, minced garlic, chopped fresh mint, salt, and pepper in a small bowl.
6. With the yoghurt sauce and lemon wedges, serve the grilled eggplant pieces.

NUTRITIONAL FACTS (PER SERVING)

Approximately 80 calories, 2g protein, 6g fat, 6g carbohydrates

ROASTED CAULIFLOWER WITH LEMON AND HERBS

Serves: 4
Prep time: 10 Minutes
Total time: 30 Minutes

INGREDIENTS

- 1 head cauliflower, cut into florets
- 2 tablespoons olive oil
- 1 tablespoon lemon juice
- 1 teaspoon dried thyme
- 1 teaspoon dried rosemary
- Salt and pepper to taste
- Lemon zest for garnish

DIRECTIONS

1. Preheat the oven to 425 degrees Fahrenheit (220 degrees Celsius).
2. Combine cauliflower florets, olive oil, lemon juice, dried thyme, dried rosemary, salt, and pepper in a large mixing basin.
3. Stir to evenly coat the cauliflower with the INGREDIENTS.
4. On a baking sheet, arrange the cauliflower in a single layer.
5. Roast the cauliflower for 20-25 Minutes, tossing once halfway through, until soft and gently browned.
6. Before serving, remove from the oven and sprinkle with lemon zest.

NUTRITIONAL FACTS (PER SERVING)

Approximately 70 calories, 3g protein, 5g fat, 6g carbohydrates

SPINACH SALAD WITH STRAWBERRIES AND GOAT CHEESE

Serves: 4
Prep time: 10 Minutes
Total time: 10 Minutes

INGREDIENTS

- 4 cups fresh spinach leaves
- 1 cup sliced strawberries
- 1/4 cup crumbled goat cheese
- 2 tablespoons chopped almonds
- 2 tablespoons balsamic vinegar
- 1 tablespoon olive oil
- Salt and pepper to taste

DIRECTIONS

1. Combine fresh spinach leaves, sliced strawberries, crumbled goat cheese, and chopped almonds in a large salad bowl.
2. In a small mixing bowl, combine the balsamic vinegar, olive oil, salt, and pepper.
3. Pour the dressing over the salad and toss lightly to coat all of the INGREDIENTS.
4. Serve immediately.

NUTRITIONAL FACTS (PER SERVING)

Approximately 100 calories, 4g protein, 7g fat, 7g carbohydrates

ZUCCHINI NOODLES WITH PESTO

Serves: 4
Prep time: 15 Minutes
Total time: 20 Minutes

INGREDIENTS

- 4 medium zucchini, spiralized into noodles
- 1/2 cup homemade or store-bought pesto
- 1/4 cup grated Parmesan cheese
- Salt and pepper to taste
- Fresh basil leaves for garnish

DIRECTIONS

1. In a large skillet, heat olive oil over medium heat.
2. Add zucchini noodles and cook for 2-3 Minutes until tender.
3. Remove from heat and add pesto to the skillet.
4. Toss to coat the zucchini noodles with the pesto sauce.
5. Sprinkle grated Parmesan cheese and season with salt and pepper.
6. Garnish with fresh basil leaves before serving.

NUTRITIONAL FACTS (PER SERVING)

Approximately 150 calories, 5g protein, 12g fat, 7g carbohydrates

QUINOA SALAD WITH ROASTED VEGETABLES

Serves: 4
Prep time: 15 Minutes
Total time: 40 Minutes

INGREDIENTS

- 1 cup quinoa
- 2 cups vegetable broth
- 1 small eggplant, diced
- 1 bell pepper, diced
- 1 zucchini, diced
- 1 red onion, sliced
- 2 tablespoons olive oil
- 2 tablespoons balsamic vinegar
- 1 teaspoon dried oregano
- Salt and pepper to taste
- Chopped fresh parsley for garnish

DIRECTIONS

1. Preheat the oven to 425 degrees Fahrenheit (220 degrees Celsius).
2. Combine the quinoa and vegetable broth in a saucepan.
3. Bring to a boil, then decrease heat to low and simmer for 15-20 Minutes until the quinoa is cooked and the liquid is absorbed.
4. In a large bowl, add chopped eggplant, bell pepper, zucchini, and sliced red onion.
5. Drizzle with olive oil, balsamic vinegar, oregano, salt, and pepper to taste.
6. Toss to evenly coat the vegetables.

7. On a baking sheet, arrange the vegetables in a single layer.
8. Roast the vegetables for 20-25 Minutes, tossing once halfway through, until soft and slightly caramelised.
9. Combine cooked quinoa and roasted vegetables in a serving bowl.
10. Mix carefully to combine all of the INGREDIENTS.
11. Before serving, garnish with fresh parsley.

NUTRITIONAL FACTS (PER SERVING)

Approximately 250 calories, 7g protein, 10g fat, 35g carbohydrates

STEAMED GREEN BEANS WITH ALMONDS

Serves: 4
Prep time: 10 Minutes
Total time: 15 Minutes

INGREDIENTS

- 1 pound green beans, trimmed
- 2 tablespoons sliced almonds
- 1 tablespoon olive oil
- 1 tablespoon lemon juice
- Salt and pepper to taste

DIRECTIONS

1. Steam the green beans until tender, about 5-7 Minutes.
2. In a small skillet, toast sliced almonds over medium heat until lightly golden.
3. In a blending bowl, combine steamed green beans, toasted almonds, olive oil, lemon juice, salt, and pepper.
4. Toss to coat the green beans evenly with the dressing.
5. Serve warm.

NUTRITIONAL FACTS (PER SERVING)

Approximately 70 calories, 3g protein, 5g fat, 5g carbohydrates

ROASTED BEET SALAD
WITH FETA CHEESE

Serves: 4
Prep time: 15 Minutes
Total time: 1 hour 15 Minutes

INGREDIENTS

- 4 medium beets, roasted, peeled, and sliced
- 2 cups mixed salad greens
- 1/4 cup crumbled feta cheese
- 2 tablespoons balsamic vinegar
- 1 tablespoon olive oil
- Salt and pepper to taste

DIRECTIONS

1. Preheat the oven to 400 degrees Fahrenheit (200 degrees Celsius).
2. Place each beetroot on a baking sheet wrapped with foil.
3. Bake for 1 hour, or until the beets are soft.
4. Remove from the oven and set aside to cool before peeling the beets.
5. Roast the beets and cut them into thin rounds.
6. Combine mixed salad greens, sliced roasted beets, and crumbled feta cheese in a large salad dish.
7. Whisk together the balsamic vinegar, olive oil, salt, and pepper in a small basin.
8. Pour the dressing over the salad and gently toss to coat all of the INGREDIENTS.
9. Chill before serving.

NUTRITIONAL FACTS (PER SERVING)

Approximately 100 calories, 4g protein, 5g fat, 10g carbohydrates

CUCUMBER AVOCADO SALAD

Serves: 4
Prep time: 10 Minutes
Total time: 10 Minutes

INGREDIENTS

- 2 cucumbers, peeled and diced
- 1 ripe avocado, diced
- 1/4 cup chopped red onion
- 2 tablespoons chopped fresh dill
- 2 tablespoons lemon juice
- 1 tablespoon olive oil
- Salt and pepper to taste

DIRECTIONS

1. In a large bowl, combine diced cucumbers, diced avocado, chopped red onion, chopped fresh dill, lemon juice, olive oil, salt, and pepper.
2. Toss gently to mix all INGREDIENTS.
3. Serve chilled.

NUTRITIONAL FACTS (PER SERVING)

Approximately 100 calories, 2g protein, 8g fat, 7g carbohydrates

BROCCOLI SLAW WITH APPLE CIDER VINAIGRETTE

Serves: 4
Prep time: 15 Minutes
Total time: 15 Minutes

INGREDIENTS

- 4 cups broccoli slaw mix
- 1/4 cup dried cranberries
- 1/4 cup chopped walnuts
- 2 tablespoons apple cider vinegar
- 1 tablespoon Dijon mustard
- 1 tablespoon honey
- 2 tablespoons olive oil
- Salt and pepper to taste

DIRECTIONS

1. In a large bowl, combine broccoli slaw mix, dried cranberries, and chopped walnuts.
2. In a small bowl, whisk together apple cider vinegar, Dijon mustard, honey, olive oil, salt, and pepper.
3. Drizzle the dressing over the slaw mix and toss gently to coat all INGREDIENTS.
4. Serve chilled.

NUTRITIONAL FACTS (PER SERVING)

Approximately 120 calories, 2g protein, 9g fat, 9g carbohydrates

STEAMED ASPARAGUS WITH LEMON BUTTER

Serves: 4
Prep time: 10 Minutes
Total time: 15 Minutes

INGREDIENTS

- 1 pound asparagus, trimmed
- 2 tablespoons butter
- 1 tablespoon lemon juice
- Salt and pepper to taste
- Lemon zest for garnish

DIRECTIONS

1. Steam the asparagus until tender, about 5-7 Minutes.
2. In a small saucepan, melt butter over low heat.
3. Stir in lemon juice, salt, and pepper.
4. Drizzle the lemon butter over the steamed asparagus.
5. Garnish with lemon zest before serving.

NUTRITIONAL FACTS (PER SERVING)

Approximately 70 calories, 3g protein, 6g fat, 3g carbohydrates

ROASTED BRUSSELS SPROUTS WITH BACON

Serves: 4
Prep time: 15 Minutes
Total time: 35 Minutes

INGREDIENTS

- 1 pound Brussels sprouts, halved
- 4 slices bacon, cooked and crumbled
- 2 tablespoons olive oil
- 1 teaspoon garlic powder
- Salt and pepper to taste

DIRECTIONS

1. Preheat the oven to 400 degrees Fahrenheit (200 degrees Celsius).
2. Combine halved Brussels sprouts, cooked and crumbled bacon, olive oil, garlic powder, salt, and pepper in a mixing bowl.
3. Toss the Brussels sprouts with the seasonings to coat evenly.
4. On a baking sheet, arrange the Brussels sprouts in a single layer.
5. Roast the Brussels sprouts for 20-25 Minutes, tossing once halfway through, until soft and caramelised.
6. Serve hot.

NUTRITIONAL FACTS (PER SERVING)

Approximately 120 calories, 6g protein, 9g fat, 8g carbohydrates

PASTA RECIPES:

LEMON GARLIC SHRIMP PASTA

Serves: 4
Prep time: 10 Minutes
Total time: 25 Minutes

INGREDIENTS

- 8 ounces gluten-free pasta
- 1 pound shrimp, peeled and deveined
- 3 cloves garlic, minced
- 2 tablespoons olive oil
- 1 tablespoon lemon juice
- Zest of 1 lemon
- Salt and pepper to taste
- Fresh parsley, chopped (for garnish)

DIRECTIONS

1. Cook the pasta according to the instructions. Drain and set aside.
2. In a large skillet, heat the olive oil over medium heat. Add the minced garlic and sauté for 1-2 Minutes until fragrant.
3. Add the shrimp to the skillet and cook for 3-4 Minutes until pink and cooked through.
4. Add the cooked pasta to the skillet along with lemon juice, lemon zest, salt, and pepper. Toss to combine.
5. Garnish with fresh parsley and serve.

NUTRITIONAL FACTS (PER SERVING)

Approximately 350 calories, 25g protein, 9g fat, 40g carbohydrates

ZUCCHINI NOODLES WITH TOMATO BASIL SAUCE

Serves: 2
Prep time: 15 Minutes
Total time: 25 Minutes

INGREDIENTS

- 2 medium zucchini
- 2 tablespoons olive oil
- 2 cloves garlic, minced
- 1 can (14 ounces) diced tomatoes
- 1/4 cup fresh basil leaves, chopped
- Salt and pepper to taste
- Grated Parmesan cheese (optional, for serving)

DIRECTIONS

1. Using a spiralizer or a vegetable peeler, construct zucchini noodles from the zucchini. Put aside.
2. Warm the olive oil in a large skillet over medium heat. Sauté the minced garlic for 1-2 Minutes, or until fragrant.
3. Cook for 10 Minutes, stirring regularly, with the diced tomatoes in the skillet.
4. Mix in the chopped basil leaves, salt, and pepper. Cook for another 2 Minutes.
5. Toss the zucchini noodles gently in the skillet to coat with the tomato basil sauce.
6. Cook until the zucchini noodles are soft, about 2-3 Minutes.
7. If preferred, top with grated Parmesan cheese.

NUTRITIONAL FACTS (PER SERVING)

Approximately 150 calories, 4g protein, 10g fat, 12g carbohydrates

CREAMY SPINACH AND MUSHROOM PASTA

Serves: 4
Prep time: 10 Minutes
Total time: 30 Minutes

INGREDIENTS

- 8 ounces gluten-free pasta
- 2 tablespoons butter
- 1 small onion, diced
- 8 ounces mushrooms, sliced
- 2 cloves garlic, minced
- 4 cups fresh spinach leaves
- 1 cup heavy cream
- 1/4 cup grated Parmesan cheese
- Salt and pepper to taste

DIRECTIONS

1. Prepare the pasta according to the package DIRECTIONS. Set aside after draining.
2. In a large skillet, melt the butter over medium heat. Sauté the diced onion for 2-3 Minutes, or until transparent.
3. To the skillet, add the sliced mushrooms and minced garlic. 5 Minutes, or until the mushrooms are soft and caramelised.
4. Cook the fresh spinach leaves in the skillet for 2-3 Minutes, or until wilted.
5. Mix in the heavy cream and Parmesan cheese. Stir until the cheese melts and the sauce thickens.
6. Season to taste with salt and pepper.

7. Toss the cooked pasta in the skillet with the creamy spinach and mushroom sauce to coat evenly.
8. Serve immediately.

NUTRITIONAL FACTS (PER SERVING)

Approximately 400 calories, 10g protein, 20g fat, 45g carbohydrates

CHICKEN ALFREDO WITH BROCCOLI

Serves: 4
Prep time: 10 Minutes
Total time: 30 Minutes

INGREDIENTS

- 8 ounces gluten-free pasta
- 2 boneless, skinless chicken breasts, cut into strips
- 2 tablespoons olive oil
- 3 cloves garlic, minced
- 2 cups broccoli florets
- 1 cup heavy cream
- 1/2 cup grated Parmesan cheese
- Salt and pepper to taste

DIRECTIONS

1. Prepare the pasta according to the package DIRECTIONS. Set aside after draining.
2. Warm the olive oil in a large skillet over medium heat. Sauté the minced garlic for 1-2 Minutes, or until fragrant.
3. Cook the chicken strips in the skillet for 6-8 Minutes, or until cooked through.
4. Cook for a another 3-4 Minutes, or until the broccoli florets are tender-crisp.
5. Mix in the heavy cream and Parmesan cheese. Stir until the cheese melts and the sauce thickens.
6. Season to taste with salt and pepper.
7. Toss the cooked pasta in the skillet with the chicken, broccoli, and Alfredo sauce to coat evenly.

8. Serve immediately.

NUTRITIONAL FACTS (PER SERVING)

Approximately 500 calories, 30g protein, 20g fat, 50g carbohydrates

SPAGHETTI SQUASH WITH MEATBALLS

Serves: 4
Prep time: 15 Minutes
Total time: 1 hour

INGREDIENTS

- 1 large spaghetti squash
- 1 pound lean ground beef
- 1/2 cup gluten-free breadcrumbs
- 1/4 cup grated Parmesan cheese
- 1 egg, beaten
- 1 teaspoon dried oregano
- 1 teaspoon dried basil
- 2 cups marinara sauce
- Fresh basil leaves (for garnish)
- Salt and pepper to taste

DIRECTIONS

1. Preheat the oven to 400 degrees Fahrenheit (200 degrees Celsius).
2. Scoop out the seeds after cutting the spaghetti squash in half lengthwise.
3. Put the cut-side down squash halves on a baking sheet lined with parchment paper.
4. Bake for 40-50 Minutes, or until the squash is soft and strands of "spaghetti" may be easily scraped with a fork.
5. Combine the ground beef, breadcrumbs, grated Parmesan cheese, beaten egg, dried oregano, dried basil, salt, and pepper in a mixing bowl. Combine thoroughly.
6. Form the mixture into 1-inch-diameter meatballs.

7. Heat a tablespoon of olive oil in a skillet over medium heat. Cook for 8-10 Minutes, or until the meatballs are browned on all sides and cooked through.
8. In a separate saucepan, heat the marinara sauce.
9. Scrape the strands of spaghetti squash into a large serving dish. Top with the meatballs and marinara sauce.
10. Serve garnished with fresh basil leaves.

NUTRITIONAL FACTS (PER SERVING)

Approximately 350 calories, 25g protein, 15g fat, 30g carbohydrates

CAPRESE PASTA SALAD

Serves: 4
Prep time: 10 Minutes
Total time: 20 Minutes

INGREDIENTS

- 8 ounces gluten-free pasta
- 1 pint cherry tomatoes, halved
- 8 ounces fresh mozzarella balls, halved
- 1/4 cup fresh basil leaves, torn
- 2 tablespoons extra-virgin olive oil
- 2 tablespoons balsamic vinegar
- Salt and pepper to taste

DIRECTIONS

1. Cook the pasta according to the package instructions. Drain and rinse with cold water.
2. In a large bowl, combine the cooked pasta, cherry tomatoes, fresh mozzarella balls, and torn basil leaves.
3. Drizzle with extra-virgin olive oil and balsamic vinegar. Toss to coat evenly.
4. Season with salt and pepper to taste.
5. Serve chilled or at room temperature.

NUTRITIONAL FACTS (PER SERVING)

Approximately 300 calories, 10g protein, 15g fat, 35g carbohydrates

GARLIC AND HERB SHRIMP PASTA

Serves: 4
Prep time: 10 Minutes
Total time: 25 Minutes

INGREDIENTS

- 8 ounces gluten-free pasta
- 1 pound shrimp, peeled and deveined
- 4 tablespoons butter
- 4 cloves garlic, minced
- 1 tablespoon fresh parsley, chopped
- 1 tablespoon fresh basil, chopped
- 1 tablespoon fresh oregano, chopped
- Salt and pepper to taste

DIRECTIONS

1. Cook the pasta according to the package instructions. Drain and set aside.
2. In a large skillet, melt the butter over medium heat. Add the minced garlic and sauté for 1-2 Minutes until fragrant.
3. Add the shrimp to the skillet and cook for 3-4 Minutes until pink and cooked through.
4. Add the cooked pasta to the skillet along with the fresh parsley, basil, and oregano. Toss to combine.
5. Season with salt and pepper to taste.
6. Serve hot.

NUTRITIONAL FACTS (PER SERVING)

Approximately 400 calories, 25g protein, 15g fat, 40g carbohydrates

PESTO ZOODLES WITH GRILLED CHICKEN

Serves: 2
Prep time: 10 Minutes
Total time: 20 Minutes

INGREDIENTS

- 2 medium zucchini
- 2 boneless, skinless chicken breasts
- 2 tablespoons olive oil, divided
- Salt and pepper to taste
- 1/4 cup homemade or store-bought low-oxalate pesto sauce
- Grated Parmesan cheese (for serving)

DIRECTIONS

1. Using a spiralizer or a vegetable peeler, create zucchini noodles from the zucchini. Set aside.
2. Season the chicken breasts with salt, pepper, and a drizzle of olive oil.
3. Heat a grill pan or grill over medium-high heat. Cook the chicken breasts for 6-8 Minutes per side until cooked through.
4. Remove the chicken from the heat and let it rest for a few Minutes. Slice into strips.
5. In a large skillet, heat the remaining olive oil over medium heat. Add the zucchini noodles and sauté for 2-3 Minutes until tender.
6. Add the sliced grilled chicken and pesto sauce to the skillet. Toss to coat the zoodles and chicken evenly with the pesto.
7. Serve hot with grated Parmesan cheese on top.

NUTRITIONAL FACTS (PER SERVING)

Approximately 350 calories, 30g protein, 20g fat, 10g carbohydrates

LEMON GARLIC SHRIMP PASTA

Serves: 4
Prep time: 10 Minutes
Total time: 20 Minutes

INGREDIENTS

- 8 ounces gluten-free pasta
- 1 pound shrimp, peeled and deveined
- 4 tablespoons olive oil
- 4 cloves garlic, minced
- Zest and juice of 1 lemon
- Salt and pepper to taste
- Fresh parsley, chopped (for garnish)

DIRECTIONS

1. Cook the pasta according to the package instructions. Drain and set aside.
2. In a large skillet, heat the olive oil over medium heat. Add the minced garlic and sauté for 1-2 Minutes until fragrant.
3. Add the shrimp to the skillet and cook for 3-4 Minutes until pink and cooked through.
4. Add the cooked pasta to the skillet along with the lemon zest and lemon juice. Toss to coat the pasta and shrimp with the lemon garlic sauce.
5. Season with salt and pepper to taste.
6. Garnish with fresh chopped parsley before serving.

NUTRITIONAL FACTS (PER SERVING)

Approximately 350 calories, 25g protein, 15g fat, 30g carbohydrates

CREAMY TOMATO BASIL PASTA

Serves: 4
Prep time: 10 Minutes
Total time: 25 Minutes

INGREDIENTS

- 8 ounces gluten-free pasta
- 1 tablespoon olive oil
- 1 small onion, diced
- 2 cloves garlic, minced
- 1 can (14 ounces) diced tomatoes
- 1/2 cup low-oxalate chicken or vegetable broth
- 1/4 cup unsweetened almond milk (or any non-dairy milk)
- 1/4 cup fresh basil leaves, chopped
- Salt and pepper to taste
- Grated Parmesan cheese (optional, for serving)

DIRECTIONS

1. Prepare the pasta according to the package DIRECTIONS. Set aside after draining.
2. Warm the olive oil in a large skillet over medium heat. Combine the diced onion and minced garlic in a mixing bowl. Sauté the onion and garlic until transparent and aromatic.
3. Add the diced tomatoes (with their juices) and the chicken or veggie broth to the skillet. Let the flavours to mingle for 10 Minutes before serving.
4. Puree the tomato mixture with an immersion blender or a tabletop blender until smooth.
5. Return the sauce to the skillet, stirring in the almond milk and basil. Season to taste with salt and pepper.

6. Toss the cooked pasta in the skillet with the creamy tomato basil sauce to coat.
7. If preferred, top with grated Parmesan cheese.

NUTRITIONAL FACTS (PER SERVING)

Approximately 300 calories, 10g protein, 10g fat, 45g carbohydrates

BOOK 3

40+ Side Dishes, Soup and Pizza recipes for a healthy and balanced Low oxalate

diet

SIDE DISH RECIPES

ROASTED BRUSSELS SPROUTS

Serves: 4
Prep time: 10 Minutes
Total time: 35 Minutes

INGREDIENTS

- 1 pound Brussels sprouts, trimmed and halved
- 2 tablespoons olive oil
- Salt and pepper to taste

DIRECTIONS

1. Preheat the oven to 400°F (200°C).
2. In a mixing bowl, toss the Brussels sprouts with olive oil, salt, and pepper.
3. Spread the Brussels sprouts in a single layer on a baking sheet.
4. Roast in the preheated oven for 25-30 Minutes or until golden brown and tender, stirring once halfway through.
5. Serve warm.

NUTRITIONAL FACTS (PER SERVING)

Approximately 80 calories, 4g protein, 5g fat, 8g carbohydrates

STEAMED ASPARAGUS WITH LEMON

Serves: 4
Prep time: 5 Minutes
Total time: 10 Minutes

INGREDIENTS

- 1 bunch asparagus, trimmed
- 1 tablespoon lemon juice
- 1 tablespoon olive oil
- Salt and pepper to taste

DIRECTIONS

1. Place the trimmed asparagus in a steamer basket over boiling water.
2. Steam for 5 Minutes or until crisp-tender.
3. In a little bowl, whisk together the lemon juice, olive oil, salt, and pepper.
4. Drizzle the lemon mixture over the steamed asparagus.
5. Serve immediately.

NUTRITIONAL FACTS (PER SERVING)

Approximately 40 calories, 2g protein, 3g fat, 4g carbohydrates

BAKED SWEET POTATO FRIES

Serves: 4
Prep time: 10 Minutes
Total time: 30 Minutes

INGREDIENTS

- 2 large sweet potatoes, cut into fries
- 2 tablespoons olive oil
- 1 teaspoon paprika
- 1/2 teaspoon garlic powder
- Salt and pepper to taste

DIRECTIONS

1. Preheat the oven to 425°F (220°C) and line a baking sheet with parchment paper.
2. In a large bowl, toss the sweet potato fries with olive oil, paprika, garlic powder, salt, and pepper.
3. Spread the fries in a single layer on the prepared baking sheet.
4. Bake for 25-30 Minutes or until golden and crispy, flipping once halfway through.
5. Serve hot.

NUTRITIONAL FACTS (PER SERVING)

Approximately 160 calories, 2g protein, 6g fat, 26g carbohydrates

GRILLED ZUCCHINI

Serves: 4
Prep time: 10 Minutes
Total time: 20 Minutes

INGREDIENTS

- 2 large zucchini, sliced lengthwise
- 2 tablespoons olive oil
- 2 cloves garlic, minced
- 1 tablespoon chopped fresh parsley
- Salt and pepper to taste

DIRECTIONS

1. Preheat the grill to medium heat.
2. In a small bowl, combine the olive oil, minced garlic, chopped parsley, salt, and pepper.
3. Brush both sides of the zucchini slices with the olive oil mixture.
4. Place the zucchini slices on the grill and cook for 5-7 Minutes per side or until tender and lightly charred.
5. Remove from the grill and serve warm.

NUTRITIONAL FACTS (PER SERVING)

Approximately 70 calories, 2g protein, 5g fat, 6g carbohydrates

QUINOA PILAF

Serves: 4
Prep time: 10 Minutes
Total time: 25 Minutes

INGREDIENTS

- 1 cup quinoa
- 2 cups vegetable broth
- 1 tablespoon olive oil
- 1 small onion, diced
- 1 clove garlic, minced
- 1/2 cup diced carrots
- 1/2 cup diced bell peppers
- 1/2 cup frozen peas
- Salt and pepper to taste

DIRECTIONS

1. Drain the quinoa after rinsing it in cold water.
2. In a saucepan, bring the vegetable broth to a boil. Reduce the heat to low and add the quinoa. Simmer for 15 Minutes, or until the liquid has been absorbed and the quinoa is tender.
3. Heat the olive oil in a separate skillet over medium heat. Sauté the diced onion and garlic until aromatic and transparent.
4. To the skillet, add the diced carrots, bell peppers, and frozen peas. Sauté until the vegetables are soft, about 5-7 Minutes.
5. Using a fork, fluff the cooked quinoa and add it to the skillet with the cooked vegetables. To blend, stir everything together.
6. Season to taste with salt and pepper.
7. Serve hot.

NUTRITIONAL FACTS (PER SERVING)

Approximately 200 calories, 6g protein, 4g fat, 35g carbohydrates
10g fat, 8g carbohydrates

CAULIFLOWER RICE

Serves: 4
Prep time: 10 Minutes
Total time: 20 Minutes

INGREDIENTS

- 1 head cauliflower, grated or processed into rice-like consistency
- 2 tablespoons olive oil
- 1 small onion, diced
- 2 cloves garlic, minced
- 1/2 cup diced bell peppers
- 1/2 cup diced carrots
- 1/2 cup frozen peas
- Salt and pepper to taste

DIRECTIONS

1. Heat the olive oil in a large skillet over medium heat. Add the diced onion and minced garlic. Sauté until fragrant and translucent.
2. Add the diced bell peppers, carrots, and frozen peas to the skillet. Cook for 5-7 Minutes or until the vegetables are tender.
3. Add the cauliflower rice to the skillet and stir to combine with the vegetables.
4. Season with salt and pepper to taste.
5. Cook for an additional 5 Minutes, stirring occasionally, until the cauliflower rice is cooked through.
6. Serve hot.

NUTRITIONAL FACTS (PER SERVING)

Approximately 60 calories, 2g protein, 4g fat, 6g carbohydrates

OVEN-ROASTED CAULIFLOWER

Serves: 4
Prep time: 10 Minutes
Total time: 30 Minutes

INGREDIENTS

- 1 head cauliflower, cut into florets
- 2 tablespoons olive oil
- 1 teaspoon paprika
- ½ teaspoon garlic powder
- Salt and pepper to taste

DIRECTIONS

1. Preheat the oven to 425°F (220°C) and line a baking sheet with parchment paper.
2. In a large bowl, toss the cauliflower florets with olive oil, paprika, garlic powder, salt, and pepper.
3. Spread the cauliflower in a single layer on the prepared baking sheet.
4. Roast in the preheated oven for 25-30 Minutes or until golden and crispy, stirring once halfway through.
5. Serve hot.

NUTRITIONAL FACTS (PER SERVING)

Approximately 70 calories, 2g protein, 5g fat, 6g carbohydrates

SAUTÉED SPINACH WITH GARLIC

Serves: 4
Prep time: 5 Minutes
Total time: 10 Minutes

INGREDIENTS

- 1 pound fresh spinach
- 2 tablespoons olive oil
- 2 cloves garlic, minced
- Salt and pepper to taste

DIRECTIONS

1. Heat the olive oil in a large skillet over medium heat. Add the minced garlic and sauté for 1 minute until fragrant.
2. Add the fresh spinach to the skillet, in batches if necessary, and toss with tongs until wilted.
3. Season with salt and pepper to taste.
4. Cook for an additional 2-3 Minutes until the spinach is heated through.
5. Serve hot.

NUTRITIONAL FACTS (PER SERVING)

Approximately 50 calories, 3g protein, 4g fat, 3g carbohydrates

BAKED PARMESAN ZUCCHINI ROUNDS

Serves: 4
Prep time: 10 Minutes
Total time: 25 Minutes

INGREDIENTS

- 2 medium zucchini, sliced into rounds
- ¼ cup grated Parmesan cheese
- ¼ cup breadcrumbs
- ½ teaspoon dried basil
- ½ teaspoon dried oregano
- ¼ teaspoon garlic powder
- Salt and pepper to taste
- Olive oil cooking spray

DIRECTIONS

1. Preheat the oven to 425°F (220°C) and line a baking sheet with parchment paper.
2. In a shallow bowl, combine the grated Parmesan cheese, breadcrumbs, dried basil, dried oregano, garlic powder, salt, and pepper.
3. Spray the zucchini rounds lightly with olive oil cooking spray on both sides.
4. Dip each zucchini round into the Parmesan breadcrumb mixture, pressing gently to adhere the coating.
5. Place the coated zucchini rounds on the prepared baking sheet in a single layer.

6. Bake for 15-20 Minutes or until the zucchini is tender and the coating is crispy and golden brown.
7. Serve hot.

NUTRITIONAL FACTS (PER SERVING)

Approximately 90 calories, 4g protein, 4g fat, 10g carbohydrates

OVEN-ROASTED BROCCOLI

Serves: 4
Prep time: 10 Minutes
Total time: 25 Minutes

INGREDIENTS

- 1 pound broccoli florets
- 2 tablespoons olive oil
- 1 teaspoon garlic powder
- ½ teaspoon smoked paprika
- Salt and pepper to taste

DIRECTIONS

1. Preheat the oven to 425°F (220°C) and line a baking sheet with parchment paper.
2. In a large bowl, toss the broccoli florets with olive oil, garlic powder, smoked paprika, salt, and pepper.
3. Spread the broccoli in a single layer on the prepared baking sheet.
4. Roast in the preheated oven for 20-25 Minutes or until the broccoli is crisp-tender and slightly charred around the edges.
5. Serve hot.

NUTRITIONAL FACTS (PER SERVING)

Approximately 60 calories, 3g protein, 4g fat, 6g carbohydrates

CAPRESE SALAD SKEWERS

Serves: 4
Prep time: 15 Minutes
Total time: 15 Minutes

INGREDIENTS

- 1 pint cherry tomatoes
- 8 small fresh mozzarella balls
- 16 fresh basil leaves
- Balsamic glaze, for drizzling
- Salt and pepper to taste
- Wooden skewers

DIRECTIONS

1. Rinse the cherry tomatoes and pat them dry.
2. Thread a cherry tomato onto a wooden skewer, followed by a fresh mozzarella ball and a fresh basil leaf. Repeat the pattern until the skewer is filled.
3. Arrange the skewers on a serving platter.
4. Drizzle balsamic glaze over the skewers.
5. Season with salt and pepper to taste.
6. Serve at room temperature.

NUTRITIONAL FACTS (PER SERVING)

Approximately 120 calories, 8g protein, 7g fat, 6g carbohydrates

ROASTED GARLIC MUSHROOMS

Serves: 4
Prep time: 10 Minutes
Total time: 30 Minutes

INGREDIENTS

- 1 pound mushrooms, cleaned and quartered
- 3 tablespoons olive oil
- 4 cloves garlic, minced
- 1 tablespoon chopped fresh parsley
- Salt and pepper to taste

DIRECTIONS

1. Preheat the oven to 400°F (200°C) and line a baking sheet with parchment paper.
2. In a large bowl, toss the mushrooms with olive oil, minced garlic, chopped parsley, salt, and pepper.
3. Spread the mushrooms in a single layer on the prepared baking sheet.
4. Roast in the preheated oven for 25-30 Minutes or until the mushrooms are golden brown and tender, stirring once halfway through.
5. Serve hot.

NUTRITIONAL FACTS (PER SERVING)

Approximately 80 calories, 3g protein, 7g fat, 4g carbohydrates

CUCUMBER TOMATO SALAD

Serves: 4
Prep time: 10 Minutes
Total time: 10 Minutes

INGREDIENTS

- 2 cucumbers, diced
- 2 tomatoes, diced
- ½ small red onion, thinly sliced
- 2 tablespoons chopped fresh parsley
- 1 tablespoon chopped fresh dill
- 2 tablespoons olive oil
- 1 tablespoon lemon juice
- Salt and pepper to taste

DIRECTIONS

1. In a large bowl, combine the diced cucumbers, tomatoes, red onion, chopped parsley, and chopped dill.
2. In a separate small bowl, whisk together the olive oil, lemon juice, salt, and pepper.
3. Pour the dressing over the cucumber and tomato mixture.
4. Toss to coat the vegetables evenly.
5. Refrigerate for at least 30 Minutes before serving to allow the flavors to meld together.
6. Serve chilled.

NUTRITIONAL FACTS (PER SERVING)

Approximately 70 calories, 2g protein, 5g fat, 6g carbohydrates

LEMON GARLIC ROASTED POTATOES

Serves: 4
Prep time: 10 Minutes
Total time: 45 Minutes

INGREDIENTS

- 1 pound baby potatoes, halved
- 2 tablespoons olive oil
- 2 cloves garlic, minced
- 1 tablespoon lemon juice
- 1 teaspoon dried thyme
- Salt and pepper to taste

DIRECTIONS

1. Preheat the oven to 400°F (200°C) and line a baking sheet with parchment paper.
2. In a large bowl, toss the halved baby potatoes with olive oil, minced garlic, lemon juice, dried thyme, salt, and pepper.
3. Spread the potatoes in a single layer on the prepared baking sheet.
4. Roast in the preheated oven for 35-40 Minutes or until the potatoes are golden brown and crispy, stirring once halfway through.
5. Serve hot.

NUTRITIONAL FACTS (PER SERVING)

Approximately 140 calories, 2g protein, 5g fat, 23g carbohydrates

SAUTEED CABBAGE WITH BACON

Serves: 4
Prep time: 10 Minutes
Total time: 25 Minutes

INGREDIENTS

- 4 slices bacon, chopped
- 1 small head cabbage, thinly sliced
- 1 small onion, thinly sliced
- 2 cloves garlic, minced
- 1 teaspoon paprika
- Salt and pepper to taste

DIRECTIONS

1. In a large skillet, cook the chopped bacon over medium heat until crispy.
2. Remove the bacon from the skillet and set aside, leaving the bacon grease in the skillet.
3. Add the thinly sliced cabbage and onion to the skillet. Sauté for 5-7 Minutes or until the cabbage is wilted and the onion is translucent.
4. Add the minced garlic, paprika, salt, and pepper to the skillet. Stir to combine.
5. Cook for an additional 2-3 Minutes until the flavors meld together.
6. Sprinkle the cooked bacon over the sautéed cabbage.
7. Serve hot.

NUTRITIONAL FACTS (PER SERVING)

Approximately 120 calories, 5g protein, 7g fat, 12g carbohydrates

ROASTED ASPARAGUS WITH LEMON

Serves: 4
Prep time: 5 Minutes
Total time: 15 Minutes

INGREDIENTS

- 1 pound asparagus spears, trimmed
- 2 tablespoons olive oil
- 1 tablespoon lemon juice
- 1 teaspoon lemon zest
- Salt and pepper to taste

DIRECTIONS

1. Preheat the oven to 425°F (220°C) and line a baking sheet with parchment paper.
2. Place the trimmed asparagus spears on the prepared baking sheet.
3. Drizzle the olive oil and lemon juice over the asparagus.
4. Sprinkle the lemon zest, salt, and pepper evenly over the asparagus.
5. Toss the asparagus to coat it evenly in the olive oil and seasonings.
6. Roast in the preheated oven for 10-12 Minutes or until the asparagus is tender and lightly charred.
7. Serve hot.

NUTRITIONAL FACTS (PER SERVING)

Approximately 70 calories, 3g protein, 5g fat, 5g carbohydrates

GREEK SALAD

Serves: 4
Prep time: 15 Minutes
Total time: 15 Minutes

INGREDIENTS

- 2 large tomatoes, diced
- 1 cucumber, diced
- ½ small red onion, thinly sliced
- ½ cup Kalamata olives, pitted and halved
- ½ cup crumbled feta cheese
- 2 tablespoons extra-virgin olive oil
- 1 tablespoon lemon juice
- 1 teaspoon dried oregano
- Salt and pepper to taste

DIRECTIONS

1. In a large bowl, combine the diced tomatoes, cucumber, red onion, Kalamata olives, and crumbled feta cheese.
2. In a separate small bowl, whisk together the extra-virgin olive oil, lemon juice, dried oregano, salt, and pepper.
3. Pour the dressing over the salad INGREDIENTS.
4. Toss to coat the vegetables and feta cheese evenly.
5. Serve chilled.

NUTRITIONAL FACTS (PER SERVING)

Approximately 170 calories, 5g protein, 13g fat, 10g carbohydrates

STEAMED ASPARAGUS WITH HOLLANDAISE SAUCE

Serves: 4
Prep time: 5 Minutes
Total time: 15 Minutes

INGREDIENTS

- 1 pound asparagus spears, trimmed
- Salt for boiling water
- Hollandaise sauce:
- 3 large egg yolks
- 1 tablespoon lemon juice
- ½ cup unsalted butter, melted
- Salt and pepper to taste
- Dash of cayenne pepper (optional)

DIRECTIONS

1. Bring a pot of salted water to a boil. Add the trimmed asparagus spears and cook for 3-4 Minutes or until tender-crisp. Drain the asparagus and set aside.
2. In a heatproof bowl, whisk together the egg yolks and lemon juice.
3. Place the bowl over a pot of simmering water, making sure the bottom of the bowl doesn't touch the water.
4. Continue whisking the egg yolk mixture until it thickens and doubles in volume, about 3-4 Minutes.
5. Slowly drizzle in the melted butter while whisking continuously until the sauce thickens further.
6. Remove the bowl from the heat and season the hollandaise sauce with salt, pepper, and cayenne pepper if desired.

7. Arrange the steamed asparagus on a serving platter and drizzle the hollandaise sauce over the top.
8. Serve immediately.

NUTRITIONAL FACTS (PER SERVING)

Approximately 180 calories, 6g protein, 18g fat, 3g carbohydrates

QUINOA PILAF WITH MIXED VEGETABLES

Serves: 4
Prep time: 10 Minutes
Total time: 25 Minutes

INGREDIENTS

- 1 cup quinoa
- 2 cups vegetable broth
- 1 tablespoon olive oil
- 1 small onion, diced
- 1 small carrot, diced
- 1 small zucchini, diced
- ½ cup frozen corn kernels
- ½ cup frozen green peas
- 1 teaspoon dried thyme
- Salt and pepper to taste

DIRECTIONS

1. Rinse the quinoa under cold water and drain well.
2. In a saucepan, bring the vegetable broth to a boil. Add the rinsed quinoa and reduce the heat to low. Cover the saucepan and simmer for 15 Minutes or until the quinoa is cooked and the liquid is absorbed.
3. In a large skillet, heat the olive oil over medium heat. Add the diced onion, carrot, and zucchini. Sauté for 5-7 Minutes or until the vegetables are tender.
4. Add the frozen corn kernels, frozen green peas, dried thyme, salt, and pepper to the skillet. Stir to combine.
5. Cook for an additional 2-3 Minutes until the vegetables are heated through.

6. Fluff the cooked quinoa with a fork and add it to the skillet with the mixed vegetables. Stir to combine.
7. Cook for another 2-3 Minutes to allow the flavors to meld together.
8. Serve hot.

NUTRITIONAL FACTS (PER SERVING)

Approximately 220 calories, 7g protein, 5g fat, 38g carbohydrates

SOUP RECIPES

CHICKEN AND VEGETABLE SOUP

Serves: 4
Prep time: 15 Minutes
Total time: 45 Minutes

INGREDIENTS

- 1 tablespoon olive oil
- 1 onion, diced
- 2 cloves garlic, minced
- 2 carrots, diced
- 2 celery stalks, diced
- 4 cups low-sodium chicken broth
- 2 cups cooked chicken breast, shredded
- 1 teaspoon dried thyme
- Salt and pepper to taste

DIRECTIONS

1. Heat the olive oil in a large pot over medium heat. Add the diced onion and minced garlic. Sauté until the onion becomes translucent.
2. Add the diced carrots and celery to the pot. Cook for 5 Minutes or until the vegetables begin to soften.
3. Pour in the chicken broth and bring to a boil. Reduce the heat to low and simmer for 20 Minutes.
4. Add the shredded chicken and dried thyme to the pot. Season with salt and pepper to taste. Simmer for an additional 10 Minutes.
5. Serve hot.

NUTRITIONAL FACTS (PER SERVING)

Approximately 180 calories, 20g protein, 5g fat, 12g carbohydrates

SPINACH AND WHITE BEAN SOUP

Serves: 4
Prep time: 10 Minutes
Total time: 30 Minutes

INGREDIENTS

- 1 tablespoon olive oil
- 1 onion, diced
- 2 cloves garlic, minced
- 4 cups low-sodium vegetable broth
- 2 cups fresh spinach
- 1 can (15 ounces) white beans, drained and rinsed
- 1 teaspoon dried oregano
- Salt and pepper to taste

DIRECTIONS

1. Heat the olive oil in a large pot over medium heat. Add the diced onion and minced garlic. Sauté until the onion becomes translucent.
2. Pour in the vegetable broth and bring to a boil. Add the fresh spinach and cook until wilted.
3. Stir in the white beans and dried oregano. Season with salt and pepper to taste. Simmer for 10 Minutes.
4. Serve hot.

NUTRITIONAL FACTS (PER SERVING)

Approximately 150 calories, 8g protein, 4g fat, 22g carbohydrates

CREAMY BROCCOLI SOUP

Serves: 4
Prep time: 10 Minutes
Total time: 30 Minutes

INGREDIENTS

- 2 cups broccoli florets
- 1 tablespoon olive oil
- 1 onion, diced
- 2 cloves garlic, minced
- 4 cups low-sodium vegetable broth
- 1 cup unsweetened almond milk
- Salt and pepper to taste

DIRECTIONS

1. Steam the broccoli florets until tender.
2. Heat the olive oil in a large pot over medium heat. Add the diced onion and minced garlic. Sauté until the onion becomes translucent.
3. Pour in the vegetable broth and bring to a boil. Add the steamed broccoli and cook for 5 Minutes.
4. Use an immersion blender or transfer the soup to a blender to puree until smooth.
5. Return the soup to the pot and stir in the almond milk. Season with salt and pepper to taste. Simmer for 5 Minutes.
6. Serve hot.

NUTRITIONAL FACTS (PER SERVING)

Approximately 120 calories, 4g protein, 7g fat, 12g carbohydrates

LENTIL SOUP

Serves: 6
Prep time: 10 Minutes
Total time: 50 Minutes

INGREDIENTS

- 1 tablespoon olive oil
- 1 onion, diced
- 2 cloves garlic, minced
- 2 carrots, diced
- 2 celery stalks, diced
- 1 cup dried lentils, rinsed
- 6 cups low-sodium vegetable broth
- 1 teaspoon dried thyme
- Salt and pepper to taste

DIRECTIONS

1. Heat the olive oil in a large pot over medium heat. Add the diced onion and minced garlic. Sauté until the onion becomes translucent.
2. Add the diced carrots and celery to the pot. Cook for 5 Minutes or until the vegetables begin to soften.
3. Stir in the dried lentils, vegetable broth, dried thyme, salt, and pepper. Bring to a boil, then reduce the heat to low and simmer for 35-40 Minutes or until the lentils are tender.
4. Serve hot.

NUTRITIONAL FACTS (PER SERVING)

Approximately 200 calories, 12g protein, 3g fat, 32g carbohydrates

TOMATO BASIL SOUP

Serves: 4
Prep time: 10 Minutes
Total time: 30 Minutes

INGREDIENTS

- 1 tablespoon olive oil
- 1 onion, diced
- 2 cloves garlic, minced
- 2 cans (14 ounces each) diced tomatoes
- 2 cups low-sodium vegetable broth
- 1/4 cup chopped fresh basil
- Salt and pepper to taste

DIRECTIONS

1. Heat the olive oil in a large pot over medium heat. Add the diced onion and minced garlic. Sauté until the onion becomes translucent.
2. Add the diced tomatoes (with their juice) and vegetable broth to the pot. Bring to a boil, then reduce the heat to low and simmer for 15 Minutes.
3. Use an immersion blender or transfer the soup to a blender to puree until smooth.
4. Stir in the chopped fresh basil. Season with salt and pepper to taste. Simmer for 5 Minutes.
5. Serve hot.

NUTRITIONAL FACTS (PER SERVING)

Approximately 100 calories, 3g protein, 3g fat, 16g carbohydrates

MUSHROOM BARLEY SOUP

Serves: 6
Prep time: 10 Minutes
Total time: 1 hour

INGREDIENTS

- 1 tablespoon olive oil
- 1 onion, diced
- 2 cloves garlic, minced
- 8 ounces mushrooms, sliced
- 1 carrot, diced
- 1 celery stalk, diced
- 1/2 cup pearl barley
- 6 cups low-sodium vegetable broth
- 1 teaspoon dried thyme
- Salt and pepper to taste

DIRECTIONS

1. Heat the olive oil in a large pot over medium heat. Add the diced onion and minced garlic. Sauté until the onion becomes translucent.
2. Add the sliced mushrooms, diced carrot, and diced celery to the pot. Cook for 5 Minutes or until the vegetables begin to soften.
3. Stir in the pearl barley, vegetable broth, dried thyme, salt, and pepper. Bring to a boil, then reduce the heat to low and simmer for 45-50 Minutes or until the barley is tender.
4. Serve hot.

NUTRITIONAL FACTS (PER SERVING)

Approximately 150 calories, 5g protein, 3g fat, 28g carbohydrates

ZUCCHINI SOUP

Serves: 4
Prep time: 10 Minutes
Total time: 30 Minutes

INGREDIENTS

- 1 tablespoon olive oil
- 1 onion, diced
- 2 cloves garlic, minced
- 3 zucchini, chopped
- 4 cups low-sodium vegetable broth
- 1/2 teaspoon dried basil
- Salt and pepper to taste

DIRECTIONS

1. Heat the olive oil in a large pot over medium heat. Add the diced onion and minced garlic. Sauté until the onion becomes translucent.
2. Add the chopped zucchini to the pot. Cook for 5 Minutes or until the zucchini begins to soften.
3. Pour in the vegetable broth and bring to a boil. Reduce the heat to low and simmer for 15 Minutes.
4. Use an immersion blender or transfer the soup to a blender to puree until smooth.
5. Stir in the dried basil. Season with salt and pepper to taste. Simmer for 5 Minutes.
6. Serve hot.

NUTRITIONAL FACTS (PER SERVING)

Approximately 80 calories, 3g protein, 4g fat, 10g carbohydrates

BUTTERNUT SQUASH SOUP

Serves: 4
Prep time: 15 Minutes
Total time: 45 Minutes

INGREDIENTS

- 1 butternut squash, peeled, seeded, and cubed
- 1 tablespoon olive oil
- 1 onion, diced
- 2 cloves garlic, minced
- 4 cups low-sodium vegetable broth
- 1/2 teaspoon ground cinnamon
- 1/4 teaspoon ground nutmeg
- Salt and pepper to taste

DIRECTIONS

1. Preheat the oven to 400°F (200°C). Place the cubed butternut squash on a baking sheet and drizzle with olive oil. Toss to coat evenly. Roast for 25-30 Minutes or until the squash is tender and lightly browned.
2. In a large pot, heat the olive oil over medium heat. Add the diced onion and minced garlic. Sauté until the onion becomes translucent.
3. Add the roasted butternut squash to the pot. Pour in the vegetable broth and bring to a boil. Reduce the heat to low and simmer for 10 Minutes.
4. Use an immersion blender or transfer the soup to a blender to puree until smooth.

5. Stir in the ground cinnamon, ground nutmeg, salt, and pepper. Simmer for an additional 5 Minutes.
6. Serve hot.

NUTRITIONAL FACTS (PER SERVING)

Approximately 150 calories, 3g protein, 5g fat, 25g carbohydrates

RED LENTIL SOUP

Serves: 6
Prep time: 10 Minutes
Total time: 40 Minutes

INGREDIENTS

- 1 tablespoon olive oil
- 1 onion, diced
- 2 cloves garlic, minced
- 1 carrot, diced
- 1 celery stalk, diced
- 1 cup red lentils, rinsed
- 6 cups low-sodium vegetable broth
- 1 teaspoon ground cumin
- Salt and pepper to taste

DIRECTIONS

1. Heat the olive oil in a large pot over medium heat. Add the diced onion and minced garlic. Sauté until the onion becomes translucent.
2. Add the diced carrot and diced celery to the pot. Cook for 5 Minutes or until the vegetables begin to soften.
3. Stir in the red lentils, vegetable broth, ground cumin, salt, and pepper. Bring to a boil, then reduce the heat to low and simmer for 25-30 Minutes or until the lentils are tender.
4. Serve hot.

NUTRITIONAL FACTS (PER SERVING)

Approximately 180 calories, 10g protein, 3g fat, 28g carbohydrates

CAULIFLOWER SOUP

Serves: 4
Prep time: 10 Minutes
Total time: 30 Minutes

INGREDIENTS

- 1 tablespoon olive oil
- 1 onion, diced
- 2 cloves garlic, minced
- 1 head cauliflower, chopped
- 4 cups low-sodium vegetable broth
- 1/2 cup unsweetened almond milk
- Salt and pepper to taste

DIRECTIONS

1. Heat the olive oil in a large pot over medium heat. Add the diced onion and minced garlic. Sauté until the onion becomes translucent.
2. Add the chopped cauliflower to the pot. Cook for 5 Minutes or until the cauliflower begins to soften.
3. Pour in the vegetable broth and bring to a boil. Reduce the heat to low and simmer for 15 Minutes or until the cauliflower is tender.
4. Use an immersion blender or transfer the soup to a blender to puree until smooth.
5. Stir in the almond milk. Season with salt and pepper to taste. Simmer for 5 Minutes.
6. Serve hot.

NUTRITIONAL FACTS (PER SERVING)

Approximately 90 calories, 3g protein, 4g fat, 12g carbohydrates

PIZZA RECIPES

MARGHERITA PIZZA

Serves: 4
Prep time: 15 Minutes
Total time: 25 Minutes

INGREDIENTS

- 1 pre-made pizza crust
- 1 cup low oxalate tomato sauce
- 1 cup shredded low oxalate mozzarella cheese
- Fresh basil leaves, for garnish

DIRECTIONS

1. Preheat the oven according to the pizza crust instructions.
2. Spread the tomato sauce evenly over the pizza crust.
3. Sprinkle the shredded mozzarella cheese over the sauce.
4. Bake in the preheated oven for the recommended time or until the cheese is melted and bubbly.
5. Remove from the oven and let it cool slightly.
6. Garnish with fresh basil leaves.
7. Slice and serve.

NUTRITIONAL FACTS (PER SERVING)

Approximately 250 calories, 12g protein, 9g fat, 30g carbohydrates

MEDITERRANEAN VEGGIE PIZZA

Serves: 4
Prep time: 20 Minutes
Total time: 35 Minutes

INGREDIENTS

- 1 pre-made pizza crust
- 1/2 cup low oxalate tomato sauce
- 1 cup sliced zucchini
- 1/2 cup sliced black olives
- 1/4 cup chopped red onion
- 1/2 cup crumbled low oxalate feta cheese
- Fresh oregano leaves, for garnish

DIRECTIONS

1. Preheat the oven according to the pizza crust instructions.
2. Spread the tomato sauce evenly over the pizza crust.
3. Arrange the sliced zucchini, black olives, and red onion on top of the sauce.
4. Sprinkle the crumbled feta cheese over the vegetables.
5. Bake in the preheated oven for the recommended time or until the crust is golden and the cheese is melted.
6. Remove from the oven and let it cool slightly.
7. Garnish with fresh oregano leaves.
8. Slice and serve.

NUTRITIONAL FACTS (PER SERVING)

Approximately 280 calories, 10g protein, 11g fat, 35g carbohydrates

BBQ CHICKEN PIZZA

Serves: 4
Prep time: 20 Minutes
Total time: 35 Minutes

INGREDIENTS

- 1 pre-made pizza crust
- 1/2 cup low oxalate barbecue sauce
- 1 cup cooked and shredded low oxalate chicken breast
- 1/4 cup thinly sliced red onion
- 1/2 cup shredded low oxalate mozzarella cheese
- Fresh cilantro leaves, for garnish

DIRECTIONS

1. Preheat the oven according to the pizza crust instructions.
2. Spread the barbecue sauce evenly over the pizza crust.
3. Sprinkle the shredded chicken and red onion over the sauce.
4. Top with shredded mozzarella cheese.
5. Bake in the preheated oven for the recommended time or until the crust is crispy and the cheese is melted.
6. Remove from the oven and let it cool slightly.
7. Garnish with fresh cilantro leaves.
8. Slice and serve.

NUTRITIONAL FACTS (PER SERVING)

Approximately 300 calories, 22g protein, 10g fat, 32g carbohydrates

SPINACH AND MUSHROOM PIZZA

Serves: 4
Prep time: 15 Minutes
Total time: 30 Minutes

INGREDIENTS

- 1 pre-made pizza crust
- 1/2 cup low oxalate tomato sauce
- 2 cups fresh spinach leaves
- 1 cup sliced mushrooms
- 1/4 cup sliced black olives
- 1/2 cup shredded low oxalate mozzarella cheese
- 1/4 cup grated Parmesan cheese

DIRECTIONS

1. Preheat the oven according to the pizza crust instructions.
2. Spread the tomato sauce evenly over the pizza crust.
3. Layer the fresh spinach leaves, sliced mushrooms, and black olives on top of the sauce.
4. Sprinkle the shredded mozzarella cheese and grated Parmesan cheese over the vegetables.
5. Bake in the preheated oven for the recommended time or until the cheese is melted and golden.
6. Remove from the oven and let it cool slightly.
7. Slice and serve.

NUTRITIONAL FACTS (PER SERVING)

Approximately 230 calories, 12g protein, 7g fat, 30g carbohydrates

GREEK PIZZA

Serves: 4
Prep time: 20 Minutes
Total time: 35 Minutes

INGREDIENTS

- 1 pre-made pizza crust
- 1/2 cup low oxalate tomato sauce
- 1 cup chopped tomatoes
- 1/2 cup sliced black olives
- 1/4 cup chopped red onion
- 1/2 cup crumbled low oxalate feta cheese
- Fresh oregano leaves, for garnish

DIRECTIONS

1. Preheat the oven according to the pizza crust instructions.
2. Spread the tomato sauce evenly over the pizza crust.
3. Scatter the chopped tomatoes, sliced black olives, and red onion on top of the sauce.
4. Sprinkle the crumbled feta cheese over the vegetables.
5. Bake in the preheated oven for the recommended time or until the crust is crispy and the cheese is melted.
6. Remove from the oven and let it cool slightly.
7. Garnish with fresh oregano leaves.
8. Slice and serve.

NUTRITIONAL FACTS (PER SERVING)

Approximately 260 calories, 10g protein, 9g fat, 35g carbohydrates

HAWAIIAN PIZZA

Serves: 4
Prep time: 15 Minutes
Total time: 30 Minutes

INGREDIENTS

- 1 pre-made pizza crust
- 1/2 cup low oxalate tomato sauce
- 1 cup diced low oxalate ham
- 1 cup diced pineapple
- 1/2 cup shredded low oxalate mozzarella cheese

DIRECTIONS

1. Preheat the oven according to the pizza crust instructions.
2. Spread the tomato sauce evenly over the pizza crust.
3. Scatter the diced ham and diced pineapple on top of the sauce.
4. Sprinkle the shredded mozzarella cheese over the toppings.
5. Bake in the preheated oven for the recommended time or until the crust is crispy and the cheese is melted.
6. Remove from the oven and let it cool slightly.
7. Slice and serve.

NUTRITIONAL FACTS (PER SERVING)

Approximately 280 calories, 14g protein, 9g fat, 35g carbohydrates

CAPRESE PIZZA

Serves: 4
Prep time: 15 Minutes
Total time: 25 Minutes

INGREDIENTS

- 1 pre-made pizza crust
- 1/2 cup low oxalate tomato sauce
- 1 cup sliced tomatoes
- 1 cup sliced low oxalate mozzarella cheese
- Fresh basil leaves, for garnish
- Balsamic glaze, for drizzling (optional)

DIRECTIONS

1. Preheat the oven according to the pizza crust instructions.
2. Spread the tomato sauce evenly over the pizza crust.
3. Arrange the sliced tomatoes on top of the sauce.
4. Place the sliced mozzarella cheese on top of the tomatoes.
5. Bake in the preheated oven for the recommended time or until the crust is crispy and the cheese is melted.
6. Remove from the oven and let it cool slightly.
7. Garnish with fresh basil leaves and drizzle with balsamic glaze, if desired.
8. Slice and serve.

NUTRITIONAL FACTS (PER SERVING)

Approximately 240 calories, 12g protein, 8g fat, 30g carbohydrates

VEGGIE SUPREME PIZZA

Serves: 4
Prep time: 20 Minutes
Total time: 35 Minutes

INGREDIENTS

- 1 pre-made pizza crust
- 1/2 cup low oxalate tomato sauce
- 1/2 cup sliced bell peppers
- 1/2 cup sliced mushrooms
- 1/4 cup sliced black olives
- 1/4 cup sliced red onion
- 1/2 cup shredded low oxalate mozzarella cheese

DIRECTIONS

1. Preheat the oven according to the pizza crust instructions.
2. Spread the tomato sauce evenly over the pizza crust.
3. Arrange the sliced bell peppers, mushrooms, black olives, and red onion on top of the sauce.
4. Sprinkle the shredded mozzarella cheese over the vegetables.
5. Bake in the preheated oven for the recommended time or until the crust is golden and the cheese is melted.
6. Remove from the oven and let it cool slightly.
7. Slice and serve.

NUTRITIONAL FACTS (PER SERVING)

Approximately 260 calories, 12g protein, 8g fat, 35g carbohydrates

MARGHERITA PIZZA

Serves: 4
Prep time: 15 Minutes
Total time: 30 Minutes

INGREDIENTS

- 1 pre-made pizza crust
- 1/2 cup low oxalate tomato sauce
- 2 cups sliced tomatoes
- 1 cup sliced low oxalate mozzarella cheese
- Fresh basil leaves, for garnish
- Olive oil, for drizzling

DIRECTIONS

1. Preheat the oven according to the pizza crust instructions.
2. Spread the tomato sauce evenly over the pizza crust.
3. Arrange the sliced tomatoes on top of the sauce.
4. Place the sliced mozzarella cheese on top of the tomatoes.
5. Bake in the preheated oven for the recommended time or until the crust is crispy and the cheese is melted.
6. Remove from the oven and let it cool slightly.
7. Garnish with fresh basil leaves and drizzle with olive oil.
8. Slice and serve.

NUTRITIONAL FACTS (PER SERVING)

Approximately 240 calories, 12g protein, 8g fat, 30g carbohydrates

MEDITERRANEAN PIZZA

Serves: 4
Prep time: 20 Minutes
Total time: 35 Minutes

INGREDIENTS

- 1 pre-made pizza crust
- 1/2 cup low oxalate tomato sauce
- 1/2 cup sliced roasted red peppers
- 1/4 cup sliced Kalamata olives
- 1/4 cup crumbled low oxalate feta cheese
- 1/4 cup chopped fresh parsley
- 1/2 teaspoon dried oregano

DIRECTIONS

1. Preheat the oven according to the pizza crust instructions.
2. Spread the tomato sauce evenly over the pizza crust.
3. Scatter the sliced roasted red peppers and Kalamata olives on top of the sauce.
4. Sprinkle the crumbled feta cheese, chopped fresh parsley, and dried oregano over the toppings.
5. Bake in the preheated oven for the recommended time or until the crust is crispy and the cheese is melted.
6. Remove from the oven and let it cool slightly.
7. Slice and serve.

NUTRITIONAL FACTS (PER SERVING)

Approximately 260 calories, 10g protein, 9g fat, 35g carbohydrates

Made in United States
North Haven, CT
06 May 2024

52204913R00107